A Trip Ab

An Account of a Journey to the Earthly Canaan and the Land of the Ancient Pharaohs; To Which Are Appended a Brief Consideration of the Geography and History of Palestine, and a Chapter on Churches of Christ in Great Britain

Don Carlos Janes

Alpha Editions

This edition published in 2024

ISBN : 9789362095312

Design and Setting By
Alpha Editions
www.alphaedis.com
Email - info@alphaedis.com

As per information held with us this book is in Public Domain.
This book is a reproduction of an important historical work. Alpha Editions uses the best technology to reproduce historical work in the same manner it was first published to preserve its original nature. Any marks or number seen are left intentionally to preserve its true form.

Contents

PREFACE. ....- 1 -
CHAPTER I. ....- 2 -
CHAPTER II. ....- 16 -
CHAPTER III. ....- 26 -
CHAPTER IV. ....- 37 -
CHAPTER V. ....- 44 -
CHAPTER VI. ....- 62 -
CHAPTER VII. ....- 72 -
CHAPTER VIII. ....- 81 -
CHAPTER IX. ....- 86 -
CHAPTER X. ....- 96 -

PREFACE.

In this volume the author has made an effort to describe his journey to Palestine and Egypt. It is his desire that the book may be interesting and instructive to its readers. The chapter on the geography of Palestine, if studied with a good map, will probably be helpful to many. The historic sketch of the land may serve as an outline of the important events in the history of that interesting country. It is desired that the last chapter may give American readers a better understanding of the work of churches of Christ in Great Britain.

This book is not a classic, but the author has tried to give a truthful account of a trip, which, to him, was full of interest and not without profit. No doubt some errors will be found, but even the critical reader may make some allowance when it is known that the writing, with the exception of a small part, was done in a period of eighty days. During this time, the writer was also engaged in evangelistic work, speaking every day without a single exception, and as often as four times on some of the days. That the careful reading of the following pages may be profitable, is the desire of THE AUTHOR.

BOWLING GREEN, KY., October 21, 1905.

CHAPTER I.

SCOTLAND AND ENGLAND.

When I was a "boy on a farm," one of my school teachers had a small machine, which was sometimes used to print the names of students in their books. Somehow I came to want a "printing press," and after a while I purchased an outfit for fifteen cents, but it was a poor thing and failed to satisfy me. Accordingly, I disposed of it and spent a larger sum for a typewriter, which was little more than a toy. This, too, was unsatisfactory, and I sold it. At a later date, I bought a second-hand typewriter, which was turned in as part payment for the machine I am now using to write this book, and now, after all these successive steps, I find myself possessed of a real typewriter. I will also mention my youthful desire for a watch. I wanted a timepiece and thought I would like for it to be of small size. I thought of it when awake, and, sometimes, when asleep, dreamed that I actually had the little watch in my possession. Since those days of dreams and disappointments, I have had three watches, and they have all been of small size.

In the same way, several years ago, I became possessed of a desire to see the Land of Promise, the earthly Canaan. I thought about it some, and occasionally spoke of it. There were seasons when the desire left me, but it would come back again. Some years ago, when I was doing evangelistic work in Canada, the desire returned—this time to stay. It grew stronger and stronger until I decided to make the trip, which was begun on the eleventh of July, 1904. After traveling many thousands of miles, seeing numerous new and interesting sights, making many pleasant acquaintances, and having a variety of experiences, I returned to the home of my father on the fourteenth day of December, having been absent five months and three days, and having had a more extensive trip than I had at first thought of taking. There is a lesson in the foregoing that I do not want overlooked. It is this: Whatever we earnestly desire is apt to be worked out in our lives. Deeds usually begin with thoughts. If the thoughts are fostered and cultivated, the deeds will probably be performed some time. It is, therefore, important that we exercise care as to the kind of thoughts we allow to remain in our hearts. "Keep thy heart with all diligence; for out of it are the issues of life" (Prov. iv. 23).

On the way to New York, I stopped in Washington and saw some of the interesting places of the National Capital. The Bureau of Engraving and Printing, where about six hundred persons were engaged in printing paper money and stamps, was visited. I also went out to the Washington Monument and climbed to the top of the winding stairs, although I might have gone up in the free elevator if I had preferred to ride. The Medical

Museum, National Museum, Treasury Building, the White House, the Capitol, and other points of interest received attention, and my short stay in this city was very enjoyable.

I spent a night in Philadelphia, after an absence of more than four years, and enjoyed a meeting with the church worshiping on Forty-sixth Street. It was very pleasant to meet those I had known when I was there before, some of whom I had been instrumental in bringing to Christ. In New York I made arrangements to sail for Glasgow on the S.S. Mongolian, of the Allan Line, which was to sail at eleven o'clock on the fourteenth of July, and the voyage was begun almost as promptly as a railway train leaves the depot. We passed the Statue of Liberty a few minutes before noon, and then I prepared some mail to be sent back by the pilot who took us down to the sea. The water was smooth almost all the way across, and we reached the desired haven on the eleventh day. I went back to my room the first morning after breakfast and was lying in my berth when a gentleman came along and told me I would have to get up, they were going to have *inspection*. I arose and found part of the crew scrubbing the floor and others washing down a wall. Everything was being put in good condition for the examination to be given by some of the officers who passed through each day at about ten o'clock. The seamen knew the inspection was sure to come, and they knew the hour at which it would take place, so they made ready for it. We know that there is a great "inspection" day appointed when God will judge the world, but we do not know the exact time. It is, therefore, important to be ready always, that the day may not overtake us "as a thief in the night."

Religious services were held on the ship each Lord's day, but I missed the last meeting. On the first Sunday morning I arose as usual and ate breakfast. As there was no opportunity to meet with brethren and break bread in memory of the Lord Jesus, I read the account of the giving of the Lord's Supper as recorded in Matthew, Mark, and John; also Paul's language concerning the institution in the eleventh chapter of the first Corinthian letter, and was thankful that my life had been spared until another beautiful resurrection morning. At half past ten o'clock I went into one of the dining rooms where two ministers were conducting a meeting. The order of the service, as nearly as I can give it, was as follows: Responsive reading of the twenty-third and twenty-fourth Psalms; prayer; the hymn, "Onward, Christian Soldiers"; reading of the twenty-ninth Psalm; prayer; the hymn, "Lead, Kindly Light"; an address on "Knowing God"; prayer; the collection, taken while singing; and the benediction. The ship furnished Bibles and hymn-books. A large copy of the Bible was placed upon a British flag at the head of one of the tables where the speaker stood, but he read from the American Revised Version of the Scriptures. The sermon was commenced by some remarks to the effect that man is hard to please. Nothing earthly satisfies him, but

Thomas expressed the correct idea when he said: "Show us the Father and it sufficeth us." The minister then went on to speak of God as "the God of patience," "the God of comfort," "the God of hope," and "the God of peace." It was, with some exceptions, a pleasing and uplifting address. There were about thirty persons in attendance, and the collection was for the Sailors' Orphans' Home in Scotland. The following is one verse of the closing hymn:

> "A few more years shall roll,
>   A few more seasons come,
> And we shall be with those that rest,
>   Asleep within the tomb;
> Then, oh, my Lord, prepare
>   My soul for that great day,
> Oh, wash me in thy precious blood
>   And take my sins away."

Before the close of the day, I read the whole of Mark's record of the life of our Savior and turned my Bible over to Gus, the steward. We had food served four times, as usual. The sea was smooth and the day passed quietly. A Catholic gentleman said something at breakfast about "saying a few prayers" to himself, and I heard a woman, in speaking about going to church, say she had beads and a prayer-book with her. Later in the day I saw her out on the deck with a novel, and what I supposed to be the prayer-book, but she was reading the novel.

Several of the passengers had reading matter with them. Some read novels, but my Book was far better than any of these. It has a greater Author, a wider range of history, more righteous laws, purer morals, and more beautiful description than theirs. It contains a longer and better love story than theirs, and reveals a much grander Hero. The Bible both moralizes and Christianizes those who permit its holy influence to move them to loving obedience of the Lord Jesus. It can fill its thoughtful reader with holy hope and lead him into the realization of that hope. It is a Book adapted to all men everywhere, and the more carefully it is read the greater the interest in it and the profit from it become. It is the volume that teaches us how to live here that we may live hereafter, and in the dying hour no one will regret having been a diligent student of its matchless pages of divine truth and wisdom.

The last Lord's day of the voyage the ship reached Moville, Ireland, where a small vessel came out and took off the passengers for Londonderry. The tilled land, visible from the ship, reminded me of a large garden. Some time that night we anchored in the harbor at Greenock, near the mouth of the River Clyde. About one o'clock the second steward came in, calling out: "Janes!" I answered from my berth and heard him call out: "Don Carlos

Janes!" Again I answered and learned that he had some mail for me. I told him to hand it in, not remembering that the door was locked, but that made no difference, for he handed it in anyhow, but the locking arrangement on that door needed repairing after he went away. I arose and examined the two pieces of mail, which were from friends, giving me directions as to where I should go when the ship got up to Glasgow, twenty-two miles from the sea. There was but one case of sea sickness reported on the whole voyage. There was one death, but the corpse was carried into port instead of being buried at sea.

The home of Brother and Sister Henry Nelmes, which was my home while I staid in Glasgow, is nicely located. Brother Nelmes and his wife are excellent people, and treated me with much kindness. Glasgow is a large and important city, with many interesting places in it. The Municipal Building with its marble stairs, alabaster balustrade, onyx columns, and other ornamentation, is attractive on the inside, but the exterior impressed me more with the idea of stability than of beauty. The old Cathedral, which I visited twice, is in an excellent state of preservation, although founded in the eleventh century. There is an extensive burial ground adjoining the Cathedral, and one of the prominent monuments is at the grave of John Knox, the reformer. These impressive words, written from memory, were spoken by the Regent at the burial of Knox, and have been carved upon his monument: "Here lieth he who never feared the face of man, who was often threatened with dag and dagger, yet hath ended his days in peace and honor." Carlyle spoke of him as a man "fearing God, without any other fear."

One day I visited the birth-place of Robert Burns, at Ayr, a point not far from Glasgow. I not only saw the "lowly thatched cottage," but a monument to the poet, "Auld Kirk Alloway," the "brig o' Doon," and many interesting articles in the museum. When the street car came to a standstill, I had the old church and cemetery on my right hand, and the monument on my left hand, while a man was standing in the road, ahead of us, blowing a cornet,—and just beyond was the new bridge over the Doon, a short distance below the old one, which is well preserved and profusely decorated with the initials of many visitors. Along the bank of "bonny Doon" lies a little garden, on the corner of which is situated a house where liquor is sold, if I mistake not. It was before this house that I saw the musician already mentioned. As I came up from the old "brig o' Doon," I saw and heard a man playing a violin near the monument. When I went down the road toward the new bridge and looked over into the garden, I saw a couple of persons executing a cake-walk, and an old man with one leg off was in the cemetery that surrounds the ruined church, reciting selections from Burns. Such is the picture I beheld when I visited this Ayrshire monument, raised in memory of the sympathetic but unfortunate Scottish poet, whose "spark o' nature's fire" has touched so many hearts that his birth-place has more visitors per annum than Shakespeare's has.

On the following day I had a pleasant boat-ride up Loch (Lake) Long, followed by a merry coach-ride across to the "bonny, bonny banks of Loch Lomond," which is celebrated in song and story. It is twenty-two miles in length and from three-quarters of a mile to five miles wide, and is called the "Queen of Scottish lakes." Ben Lomond, a mountain rising to a height of more than three thousand feet, stands on the shore, and it is said that Robert Bruce, the hero of Bannockburn, once hid himself in a cave in this mountain. A pleasant boat-ride down the lake brought me back to Glasgow in time to attend a meeting of the brethren in Coplaw Street that night.

Leaving my true friends who had so kindly entertained me in Glasgow, I proceeded to Edinburgh, the city where Robert Burns came into prominence. In the large Waverley Station a stranger, who knew of my coming through word from Brother Ivie Campbell, of Kirkcaldy, stopped me and asked: "Is your name Don Carlos Janes?" It was another good friend, Brother J.W. Murray. He said he told some one he was looking for me, and was told, in return, that he would not be able to find me. His answer to this was that he had picked out a man before, and he might pick out another one; and so he did, without any difficulty. After a little time spent in Waverley gardens, I ascended the Walter Scott Monument, which is two hundred feet high. The winding stairway is rather narrow, especially at the top, and it is not well lighted. As I was coming down the stairs, I met a lady and gentleman. The little woman was not at all enthusiastic over the experience she was having, and, without knowing of my presence, she was wondering what they would do if they were to meet any one. "Come on up and see," I said, and we passed without any special difficulty, but she said she didn't believe "two stout ones could" pass. As she went on up the winding way, she was heard expressing herself in these words: "Oh, it is a place, isn't it? I don't like it." The tourist finds many "places", and they are not all desirable. Princess Street, on which the monument is located, is the prettiest street that I have ever seen. One side is occupied by business houses and hotels, the other is a beautiful garden, where one may walk or sit down, surrounded by green grass and beautiful flowers.

Edinburgh Castle is an old fortification on the summit of a lofty hill overlooking the city. It is now used as barracks for soldiers, and is capable of accommodating twelve hundred men. Queen Mary's room is a small chamber, where her son, James the First of Scotland and the Sixth of England, was born. I was in the old castle in Glasgow where she spent the night before the Battle of Langside, and later stood by her tomb in Westminster Abbey. Her history, a brief sketch of which is given here, is interesting and pathetic. "Mary Queen of Scots was born in Linlithgow

Palace, 1542; fatherless at seven days old; became Queen December 8th, 1542, and was crowned at Stirling, September 9th, 1543; carried to France, 1548; married to the Dauphin, 1558; became Queen of France, 1559; a widow, 1560; returned to Scotland, 1561; married Lord Darnley, 1565; her son (and successor), James VI., born at Edinburgh Castle, 1566; Lord Darnley murdered, February, 1567; Mary married to the Earl of Bothwell, May, 1567, and was compelled to abdicate in favor of her infant son. She escaped from Lochleven Castle, lost the Battle of Langside, and fled to England, 1568. She was beheaded February 8th, 1587, at Fotheringay Castle, in the forty-fifth year of her age, almost nineteen years of which she passed in captivity.

"Puir Mary was born and was cradled in tears,
Grief cam' wi' her birth, and grief grew wi' her years."

In the crown-room are to be seen the regalia of Scotland, consisting of the crown, scepter, sword of state, a silver rod of office, and other jewels, all enclosed in a glass case surrounded by iron work. St. Margaret's Chapel, seventeen feet long and eleven feet wide, stands within the castle enclosure and is the oldest building in the city. A very old cannon, called Mons Meg, was brought back to the castle through the efforts of Walter Scott, and is now on exhibition. I visited the Hall of Statuary in the National Gallery, the Royal Blind Asylum, passed St. Giles Cathedral, where John Knox preached, dined with Brother Murray, and boarded the train for Kirkcaldy, where I as easily found Brother Campbell at the station as Brother Murray had found me in Edinburgh.

I had been in correspondence with Brother Campbell for some years, and our meeting was a pleasure, and my stay at Kirkcaldy was very enjoyable. We went up to St. Andrews, and visited the ruins of the old Cathedral, the University, a monument to certain martyrs, and the home of a sister in Christ. But little of the Cathedral remains to be seen. It was founded in 1159, and was the most magnificent of Scottish churches. St. Rule's Tower, one hundred and ten feet high, still stands, and we had a fine view from the top. The time to leave Kirkcaldy came too soon, but I moved on toward Wigan, England, to attend the annual meeting of churches of Christ. Brother Campbell accompanied me as far as Edinburgh, and I then proceeded to Melrose, where I stopped off and visited Abbotsford, the home of Sir Walter Scott. It is situated on the River Tweed, a short distance from Melrose, and was founded in 1811. By the expenditure of a considerable sum of money it was made to present such an appearance as to be called "a romance in stone and lime." Part of this large house is occupied as a dwelling, but some of the rooms are kept open for the numerous visitors who call from time to time. The young lady who was guide the day I was at Abbotsford, first showed us Sir Walter's study. It is a small room, with book shelves from the floor to the ceiling, the desk on which Scott wrote his novels sitting in the middle of the floor. A writing-box, made of wood taken from one of the ships of the Spanish Armada, sits on the desk, and the clothes worn by the great novelist a short time before his death are kept under glass in a case by the window, while a cast of his face is to be seen in a small room adjoining the study. We next passed into the library, which, with the books in the study, contains about twenty thousand volumes. In the armory are numerous guns, pistols, swords, and other relics. There is some fine furniture in one of the rooms, and the walls are covered with paper printed by hand in China nearly ninety years ago. Perhaps some who read these lines will recall the sad story of Genivra, who hid herself in an oaken chest in an attic, and perished there, being imprisoned by the spring lock. This oaken chest was received at Abbotsford a short time before Scott's death, and is now on exhibition. Sir Walter, as the guide repeatedly called him, spent the last years of his life under the burden of a heavy debt, but instead of making use of the bankrupt law, he set to work heroically with his pen to clear up the indebtedness. He wrote rapidly, and his books sold well, but he was one day compelled to lay down his pen before the task was done. The King of England gave him a trip to the Mediterranean, for the benefit of his health, but it was of no avail. Sir Walter returned to his home on the bank of the Tweed, and died September twenty-first, 1832. In his last illness, this great author, who had produced so many volumes that were being read then and are still being read, asked his son-in-law to read to him. The son-in-law asked what book he should read, to which Sir Walter replied: "Book? There is but one Book! Read me the Bible." In Melrose I visited the ruins of the Abbey, and then went on to Wigan.

After the annual meeting, I went to Birmingham and stayed a short while. From here I made a little journey to the birth-place of Shakespeare, at Stratford-on-Avon, a small, quiet town, where, to the best of my recollection, I saw neither street cars nor omnibuses. After being in several large cities, it was an agreeable change to spend a day in this quiet place, where the greatest writer in the English tongue spent his boyhood and the last days of his life on earth. The house where he was born was first visited. A fee of sixpence (about twelve cents) secures admission, but another sixpence is required if the library and museum are visited. The house stands as it was in the poet's early days, with a few exceptions. Since that time, however, part of it has been used as a meat market and part as an inn. In 1847, the property was announced for sale, and it fell into the hands of persons who restored it as nearly as possible to its original condition.

It has two stories and an attic, with three gables in the roof facing the street. At the left of the door by which the tourist is admitted, is a portion of the house where the valuable documents of the corporation are stored, while to the right are the rooms formerly used as the "Swan and Maidenhead Inn," now converted into a library and museum. The windows in the upstairs room where the poet was born are fully occupied with the autographs of visitors who have scratched their names there. I was told that the glass is now valuable simply as old glass, and of course the autographs enhance the value. The names of Scott and Carlyle are pointed out by the attendant in charge. From a back window one can look down into the garden, where, as far as possible, all the trees and flowers mentioned in Shakespeare's works have been planted. For some years past the average number of visitors to this house has been seven thousand a year. The poet's grave is in Trinity Church, at Stratford, beneath a stone slab in the floor bearing these lines:

"Good friend, for Jesus' sake, forbear
To digg the dust enclosed here.
Blest be ye man y spares these stones,
And curst be he ty moves my bones."

On the wall, just at hand, is a bust made from a cast taken after his death. Near by is a stained-glass window with the inscription, "America's gift to Shakespeare's church," and not far away is a card above a collection-box with an inscription which informs "visitors from U.S.A." that there is yet due on the window more than three hundred dollars. The original cost was about two thousand five hundred dollars. The Shakespeare Memorial is a small theater by the side of the Avon, with a library and picture gallery attached. The first stone was laid in 1877, and the building was opened in 1879 with a performance of "Much Ado About Nothing." The old school once attended by the poet still stands, and is in use, as is also the cottage of Anne Hathaway, situated a short distance from Stratford. I returned to Birmingham, and soon went on to Bristol and saw the orphans' homes founded by George Muller.

These homes, capable of accommodating two thousand and fifty orphans, are beautifully situated on Ashley Downs. Brother William Kempster and I visited them together, and were shown through a portion of one of the five large buildings by an elderly gentleman, neat, clean, and humble, who was sent down by the manager of the institution, a son-in-law of Mr. Muller, who died in 1898, at the advanced age of ninety-three years. We saw one of the dormitories, which was plainly furnished, but everything was neat and clean. We were also shown two dining-rooms, and the library-room in which Mr. Muller conducted a prayer-meeting only a night or two before his death. In this room we saw a fine, large picture of the deceased, and were told by the "helper" who was showing us around that Mr. Muller was accustomed to saying: "Oh, I am such a happy man!" The expression on his face in this picture is quite in harmony with his words just quoted. One of his sayings was: "When anxiety begins, faith ends; when faith begins, anxiety ends."

Mr. Muller spent seventy years of his life in England and became so thoroughly Anglicized that he wished his name pronounced "Miller." He was the founder of the "Scriptural Knowledge Institution for Home and Abroad" and was a man of much more than ordinary faith. His work began about 1834, with the distribution of literature, and the orphan work, if I mistake not, was begun two years later. "As the result of prayer to God" more than five millions of dollars have been applied for the benefit of the orphans. He never asked help of man, but made his wants known to God, and those who are now carrying on the work pursue the same course, but the collection-boxes put up where visitors can see them might be considered by some as an invitation to give. The following quotation from the founder of the orphanages will give some idea of the kind of man he was. "In carrying on this work simply through the instrumentality of prayer and faith, without applying to any human being for help, my great desire was, that it might be seen that, now, in the nineteenth century, *God is still the Living God, and now, as well as thousands of years ago, he listens to the prayers of his children and helps those who trust in him.* In all the forty-two countries through which I traveled during the twenty-one years of my missionary service, numberless instances came before me of the benefit which this orphan institution has been, in this respect, not only in making men of the world see the reality of the things of God, and by converting them, but especially by leading the children of God more abundantly to give themselves to prayer, and by strengthening their faith. *Far beyond what I at first expected to accomplish*, the Lord has been pleased to give me. But what I have *seen* as the fruit of my labor in this way may not be the thousandth part of what I *shall* see when the Lord Jesus comes again; as day by day, for sixty-one years, I have earnestly labored, in believing prayer, that God would be pleased, most abundantly, to bless this service in the way I have stated."

The objects of the Scriptural Knowledge Institution are set forth as follows: "To assist day schools and Sunday-schools in which instruction is given upon scriptural principles," etc. By day schools conducted on scriptural principles, they mean "those in which the teachers are believers; where the way of salvation is pointed out, and in which no instruction is given opposed to the principles of the Gospel." In these schools the Scriptures are read daily by the children. In the Sunday-schools the "teachers are believers, and the Holy Scriptures alone are the foundation of instruction." The second object of the Institution is "to circulate the Holy Scriptures." In one year four thousand three hundred and fifty Bibles were sold, and five hundred and twenty-five were given away; seven thousand eight hundred and eighty-one New Testament were sold, and one thousand five hundred and seventy-four were given away; fifty-five copies of the Psalms were sold, and thirty-eight were given away; two thousand one hundred and sixty-three portions of the Holy Scriptures were sold, and one hundred and sixty-two were given away; and three thousand one hundred illustrated portions of the Scriptures were given away. There have been circulated through this medium, since March, 1834, three hundred and eleven thousand two hundred and seventy-eight Bibles, and one million five hundred and seven thousand eight hundred and one copies of the New Testament. They keep in stock almost four hundred sorts of Bibles, ranging in price from twelve cents each to more than six dollars a copy.

Another object of the Institution is to aid in missionary efforts. "During the past year one hundred and eighty laborers in the Word and doctrine in various parts of the world have been assisted." The fourth object is to circulate such publications as may be of benefit both to believers and unbelievers. In a single year one million six hundred and eleven thousand two hundred and sixty-six books and tracts were distributed gratuitously. The fifth object is to board, clothe, and scientifically educate destitute orphans. Mr. Muller belonged to that class of religious people who call themselves Brethren, and are called by others "Plymouth Brethren."

After leaving Bristol, I went to London, the metropolis of the world. The first important place visited was Westminster Abbey, an old church, founded in the seventh century, rebuilt in 1049, and restored to its present form in the thirteenth century. Many eminent men and women are buried here. Chaucer, the first poet to find a resting place in the Abbey, was interred in 1400. The place where Major Andre is buried is marked by a small piece of the pavement bearing his name. On the wall close by is a monument to him. Here are the graves of Isaac Newton, Charles Dickens, Alfred Tennyson, Charles Darwin, and many others, including Kings and Queens of England for centuries. In the Poets' Corner are monuments to Coleridge, Southey, Shakespeare, Burns, Tennyson, Milton, Gray, Spencer, and others, and one bearing the inscription "O Rare Ben Jonson." There is also a bust of Longfellow, the only foreigner accorded a memorial in the Abbey. The grave of David Livingstone, the African explorer and missionary, is covered with a black stone of some kind, which forms a part of the floor or pavement, and contains an inscription in brass letters, of which the following quotation is a part: "All I can add in my solitude is, may heaven's rich blessings come down on every one, American, English, or Turk, who will help to heal this open sore of the world."

Concerning this interesting old place which is visited by more than fifty thousand Americans annually, Jeremy Taylor wrote: "Where our Kings are crowned, their ancestors lie interred, and they must walk over their grandsires to take the crown. There is an acre sown with royal seed, the copy of the greatest change, from rich to naked, from ceiled roofs to arched coffins, from living like gods to die like men. There the warlike and the peaceful, the fortunate and the miserable, the beloved and despised princes mingle their dust and pay down their symbol of mortality, and tell all the world that when we die our ashes shall be equal to Kings, and our accounts easier, and our pains for our sins shall be less." While walking about in the Abbey, I also found these lines from Walter Scott:

> "Here, where the end of earthly things
> Lays heroes, patriots, bards and kings;
> Where stiff the hand and still the tongue
> Of those who fought, and spoke, and sung;
> Here, where the fretted aisles prolong
> The distant notes of holy song,
> As if some Angel spoke again
> 'All peace on earth, good will to men';
> If ever from an English heart,
> Here let prejudice depart."

Bunhill Fields is an old cemetery where one hundred and twenty thousand burials have taken place. Here lie the ashes of Isaac Watts, the hymn writer; of Daniel De Foe, author of "Robinson Crusoe," and of John Bunyan, who in Bedford jail wrote "Pilgrim's Progress." The monuments are all plain. The one at the grave of De Foe was purchased with the contributions of seventeen hundred people, who responded to a call made by some paper. On the top of Bunyan's tomb rests the figure of a man, perhaps a representation of him whose body was laid in the grave below. On one of the monuments in this cemetery are the following words concerning the deceased: "In sixty-seven months she was tapped sixty-six times. Had taken away two hundred and forty gallons of water without ever repining at her case or ever fearing the operation."

Just across the street from Bunhill Fields stands the house once occupied by John Wesley (now containing a museum) and a meeting-house which was built in Wesley's day. The old pulpit from which Mr. Wesley preached is still in use, but it has been lowered somewhat. In front of the chapel is a statue of Wesley, and at the rear is his grave, and close by is the last resting place of the remains of Adam Clarke, the commentator.

A trip to Greenwich was quite interesting. I visited the museum and saw much of interest, including the painted hall, the coat worn by Nelson at the Battle of the Nile, and the clothing he wore when he was mortally wounded at Trafalgar. I went up the hill to the Observatory, and walked through an open door to the grounds where a gentleman informed me that visitors are not admitted without a pass; but he kindly gave me some information and told me that I was standing on the prime meridian. On the outside of the enclosure are scales of linear measure up to one yard, and a large clock.

After the trip to Greenwich, I went over the London Bridge, passed the fire monument, and came back across the Thames by the Tower Bridge, a peculiar structure, having two levels in one span, so passengers can go up the stairs in one of the towers, cross the upper level, and go down the other stairs when the lower level is opened for boats to pass up and down the river. While in Scotland, I twice crossed the great Forth Bridge, which is more than a mile and a half long and was erected at a cost of above fifteen millions of dollars. There are ten spans in the south approach, eight in the north approach, and two central spans each seventeen hundred feet long. The loftiest part of the structure is three hundred and sixty-one feet above high-water mark.

The Albert Memorial is perhaps the finest monument seen on the whole trip. The Victoria and Albert Museum contains the original Singer sewing-machine, and a printing-press supposed to have been used by Benjamin Franklin, and many other interesting things. The Natural History Museum also contains much to attract the visitor's attention. Here I saw the skeleton of a mastodon about ten feet tall and twenty feet long; also the tusks of an extinct species of Indian elephant, which were nine feet and nine inches long. There is also an elephant tusk on exhibition ten feet long and weighing two hundred and eighty pounds.

Madam Tussaud's exhibition of wax figures and relics is both interesting and instructive, and well repays one for the time and expense of a visit. Several American Presidents are represented in life-size figures, along with Kings and others who have been prominent in the affairs of men. In the Napoleon room are three of the great warrior's carriages, the one used at Waterloo being in the number. London Tower is a series of strong buildings, which have in turn served as a fortress, a palace, and a prison. I saw the site of Anne Boleyn's execution, but that which had the most interest for me was the room containing the crown jewels. They are kept in a glass case ten or twelve feet in diameter, in a small, circular room. Outside of the case there is an iron cage surrounded by a network of wire. The King's crown is at the top of the collection, which contains other crowns, scepters, swords, and different costly articles. This crown, which was first made in 1838 for Queen Victoria, was enlarged for Edward, the present King. It contains two thousand eight hundred and eighteen diamonds, two hundred and ninety-seven pearls, and many other jewels. One of the scepters is supposed to contain a part of the cross of Christ, but the supposition had no weight with me. One of the attendants told me the value of the whole collection was estimated at four million pounds, and that it would probably bring five times that much if sold at auction. As the English pound is worth about four dollars and eighty-seven cents, this little room contains a vast treasure—worth upwards of a hundred million dollars.

I will only mention Nelson's monument in Trafalgar Square, the Parliament Buildings, St. Paul's Cathedral, Kew Gardens, Hampton Court Palace, and the Zoological Gardens. I also visited the Bank of England, which "stands on ground valued at two hundred and fifty dollars per square foot. If the bank should ever find itself pressed for money, it could sell its site for thirty-two million seven hundred and seventy thousand dollars." It is a low building that is not noted for its beauty. If it were located in New York, probably one of the tall buildings characteristic of that city would be erected on the site.

The British Museum occupied my time for hours, and I shall not undertake to give a catalogue of the things I saw there, but will mention a few of them. There are manuscripts of early writers in the English tongue, including a copy of Beowulf, the oldest poem in the language; autograph works of Daniel De Foe, Ben Jonson, and others; the original articles of agreement between John Milton and Samuel Symmons relating to the sale of the copyright of "a poem entitled 'Paradise Lost.'" There was a small stone inscribed in Phoenician, with the name of Nehemiah, the son of Macaiah, and pieces of rock that were brought from the great temple of Diana at Ephesus; a fragment of the Koran; objects illustrating Buddhism in India; books printed by William Caxton, who printed the first book in English; and Greek vases dating back to 600 B.C. In the first verse of the twentieth chapter of Isaiah we have mention of "Sargon, the king of Assyria." For centuries this was all the history the world had of this king, who reigned more than seven hundred years before Christ. Within recent times his history has been dug up in making excavations in the east, and I saw one of his inscribed bricks and two very large, human-headed, winged bulls from a doorway of his palace.

The carvings from the palace of Sennacherib, tablets from the library of Asur-Banipal, and brick of Ur-Gur, king of Ur about twenty-five centuries before Christ, attracted my attention, as did also the colossal left arm of a statue of Thotmes III., which measures about nine feet. The Rosetta stone, by which the Egyptian hieroglyphics were translated, and hundreds of other objects were seen. In the mummy-room are embalmed bodies, skeletons, and coffins that were many centuries old when Jesus came to earth, some of them bearing dates as early as 2600 B.C., and in the case of a part of a body found in the third pyramid the date attached is 3633 B.C. Being weary, I sat down, and my note book contains this entry: "1:45 P.M., August 20. Resting here in the midst of mummies and sarcophagi thousands of years old."

From the top of the Monument I took a bird's-eye view of the largest of all earthly cities, or at least I looked as far as the smoky atmosphere would permit, and then returned to my stopping place at Twynholm. As I rode back on the top of an omnibus, the houses of one of the Rothschild family and the Duke of Wellington were pointed out. My sight-seeing in Scotland and England was now at an end, and the journey so far had been very enjoyable and highly profitable. I packed up and went down to Harwich, on the English Channel, where I embarked on the Cambridge for Antwerp, in Belgium. In this chapter I have purposely omitted reference to my association with the churches, as that will come up for consideration in another chapter.

CHAPTER II.

CROSSING EUROPE.

Immediately after my arrival in Antwerp I left for a short trip over the border to Rosendaal, Holland, where I saw but little more than brick-houses, tile roofs, and wooden shoes. I then returned to Antwerp, and went on to Brussels, the capital of Belgium. The battlefield of Waterloo is about nine and a half miles from Brussels, and I had an enjoyable trip to this notable place. The field is farming land, and now under cultivation. The chief object of interest is the Lion Mound, an artificial hill surmounted by the figure of a large lion. The mound is ascended by about two hundred and twenty-three steps, and from its summit one has a good view of the place where the great Napoleon met his defeat on the fifteenth of June, 1815. There is another monument on the field, which, though quite small and not at all beautiful, contains an impressive inscription. It was raised in memory of Alexander Gordon, an aide to the Duke of Wellington, and has the following words carved on one side: "A disconsolate sister and five surviving brothers have erected this simple memorial to the object of their tenderest affection."

From Brussels I went over to Aix-la-Chapelle, on the frontier of Germany, where I spent but little time and saw nothing of any great interest to me. There was a fine statue of Wilhelm I., a crucifixion monument, and, as I walked along the street, I saw an advertisement for "Henry Clay Habanna Cigarren," but not being a smoker, I can not say whether they were good or not. In this city I had an amusing experience buying a German flag. I couldn't speak "Deutsch," and she couldn't speak English, but we made the trade all right.

My next point was Paris, the capital of the French Republic, and here I saw many interesting objects. I first visited the church called the Madeleine. I also walked along the famous street *Champs Elysees,* visited the magnificent Arch of Triumph, erected to commemorate the victories of Napoleon, and viewed the Eiffel Tower, which was completed in 1889 at a cost of a million dollars. It contains about seven thousand tons of metal, and the platform at the top is nine hundred and eighty-five feet high. The Tomb of Napoleon is in the Church of the Invalides, one of the finest places I had visited up to that time. The spot where the Bastile stood is now marked by a lofty monument. The garden of the Tuileries, Napoleon's palace, is one of the pretty places in Paris. Leaving this city in the morning, I journeyed all day through a beautiful farming country, and reached Pontarlier, in southern France, for the night.

My travel in Switzerland, the oldest free state in the world, was very enjoyable. As we were entering the little republic, in which I spent two days, the train was running through a section of country that is not very rough, when, all in a moment, it passed through a tunnel overlooking a beautiful valley, bounded by mountains on the opposite side and presenting a very pleasing view. There were many other beautiful scenes as I journeyed along, sometimes climbing the rugged mountain by a cog railway, and sometimes riding quietly over one of the beautiful Swiss lakes. I spent a night at lovely Lucerne, on the Lake of the Four Cantons, the body of water on which William Tell figured long ago. Lucerne is kept very clean, and presents a pleasing appearance to the tourist.

I could have gone to Fluelin by rail, but preferred to take a boat ride down the lake, and it proved to be a pleasant and enjoyable trip. The snow could be seen lying on the tops of the mountains while the flowers were blooming in the valleys below. Soon after leaving Fluelin, the train entered the St. Gothard Tunnel and did not reach daylight again for seventeen minutes. This tunnel, at that time the longest in the world, is a little more than nine miles in length. It is twenty-eight feet wide, twenty-one feet high, lined throughout with masonry, and cost eleven million four hundred thousand dollars. Since I was in Switzerland the Simplon Tunnel has been opened. It was begun more than six years ago by the Swiss and Italian Governments, an immense force of hands being worked on each end of it. After laboring day and night for years, the two parties met on the twenty-fourth of February. This tunnel, which is double, is more than twelve miles long and cost sixteen millions of dollars.

At Chiasso we did what is required at the boundary line of all the countries visited; that is, stop and let the custom-house officials inspect the baggage. I had nothing dutiable and was soon traveling on through Italy, toward Venice, where I spent some time riding on one of the little omnibus steamers that ply on its streets of water. But not all the Venetian streets are like this, for I walked on some that are paved with good, hard sandstone. I was not moved by the beauty of the place, and soon left for Pisa, passing a night in Florence on the way. The chief point of interest was the Leaning Tower, which has eight stories and is one hundred and eighty feet high. This structure, completed in the fourteenth century, seems to have commenced to lean when the third story was built. The top, which is reached by nearly three hundred steps, is fourteen feet out of perpendicular. Five large bells are suspended in the tower, from the top of which one can have a fine view of the walled city, with its Cathedral and Baptistery, the beautiful surrounding country, and the mountains in the distance.

The next point visited was Rome, old "Rome that sat on her seven hills and from her throne of beauty ruled the world." One of the first things I saw when I came out of the depot was a monument bearing the letters "S.P.Q.R." (the Senate and the people of Rome) which are sometimes seen in pictures concerning the crucifixion of Christ. In London there are numerous public water-closets; in France also there are public urinals, which are almost too public in some cases, but here in Rome the climax is reached, for the urinals furnish only the least bit of privacy. One of them, near the railway station, is merely an indentation of perhaps six or eight inches in a straight wall right against the sidewalk, where men, women, and children are passing.

By the aid of a guide-book and pictorial plan, I crossed the city from the gateway called "Porto del Popolo" to the "Porto S. Paolo," seeing the street called the "Corso," or race course, Piazza Colonna, Fountain of Treves, Trajan's Forum, Roman Forum, Arch of Constantine, Pantheon, Colosseum, and the small Pyramid of Caius Cestus.

The Porto del Popolo is the old gateway by which travelers entered the city before the railroad was built. It is on the Flammian Way and is said to have been built first in A.D. 402. Just inside the gate is a space occupied by an Egyptian obelisk surrounded by four Egyptian lions. The Corso is almost a mile in length and extends from the gate just mentioned to the edge of the Capitoline Hill, where a great monument to Victor Emmanuel was being built. The Fountain of Treves is said to be the most magnificent in Rome, and needs to be seen to be appreciated. It has three large figures, the one in the middle representing the Ocean, the one on the left, Fertility, and the one on the right, Health. Women who are disposed to dress fashionably at the expense of a deformed body might be profited by a study of this figure of Health. Trajan's Forum is an interesting little place, but it is a small show compared with the Roman Forum, which is much more extensive, and whose ruins are more varied. The latter contains the temples of Vespasian, of Concordia, of Castor and Pollux, and others. It also contains the famous Arch of Titus, the Basilica of Constantine, the remains of great palaces, and other ruins. "Originally the Forum was a low valley among the hills, a convenient place for the people to meet and barter." The Palatine Hill was fortified by the first Romans, and the Sabines lived on other hills. These two races finally united, and the valley between the hills became the site of numerous temples and government buildings. Kings erected their palaces in the Forum, and it became the center of Roman life. But when Constantine built his capital at Constantinople, the greatness of the city declined, and it was sacked and plundered by enemies from the north. The Forum became a dumping ground for all kinds of rubbish until it was almost hidden from view, and it was called by a name signifying cow pasture. It has been partly excavated within the last century, and the ruined temples and palaces have been brought to light, making it once more a place of absorbing interest. I wandered around and over and under and through these ruins for a considerable length of time, and wrote in my note book: "There is more here than I can comprehend."

I was in a garden on top of one part of the ruins where flowers and trees were growing, and then I went down through the mass of ruins by a flight of seventy-five stairs, which, the attendant said, was built by Caligula. I was then probably not more than half way to the bottom of this hill of ruins, which is honeycombed with corridors, stairways, and rooms of various sizes. The following scrap of history concerning Caligula will probably be interesting: "At first he was lavishly generous and merciful, but he soon became mad, and his cruelty knew no bounds. He banished or murdered his relatives and many of his subjects. Victims were tortured and slain in his presence while dining, and he uttered the wish that all the Roman people had but one neck, that he might strike it off at one blow. He built a bridge across the Bay of Baiae, and planted trees upon it and built houses upon it that he might say he had crossed the sea on dry land. In the middle of the bridge he gave a banquet, and at the close had a great number of the guests thrown into the sea. He made his favorite horse a priest, then a consul, and also declared himself a god, and had temples built in his honor." It is said that Tiberius left the equivalent of one hundred and eighteen millions of dollars, and that Caligula spent it in less than a year. The attendant pointed out the corridor in which he said this wicked man was assassinated.

Near one of the entrances to the Forum stands the Arch of Titus, erected to commemorate the victory of the Romans over the Jews at Jerusalem in A.D. 70. It is built of Parian marble and still contains a well-preserved figure of the golden candlestick of the Tabernacle carved on one of its walls. There is a representation of the table of showbread near by, and some other carvings yet remain, indicating something of the manner in which the monument was originally ornamented.

The Colosseum, commenced by Vespasian in A.D. 72 and finished by Titus eight years later, is a grand old ruin. It is an open theater six hundred and twelve feet long, five hundred and fifteen feet wide, and one hundred and sixty-five feet high. This structure, capable of seating eighty-seven thousand people, stands near the bounds of the Forum. It is the largest of its kind, and is one of the best preserved and most interesting ruins in the world. When it was dedicated, the games lasted one hundred days, and five thousand wild beasts were slain. During the persecution of the Christians it is said to have been the scene of fearful barbarities.

On the second day I entered the Pantheon, "the best preserved monument of ancient Rome," built by Marcus Agrippa, and consecrated to Mars, Venus, and others. It was burned in the reign of Titus and rebuilt by Hadrian, and in A.D. 608 Pope Boniface consecrated it as a church. The interior is shaped like a vast dome, and the only opening for light is a round hole in the top. Raphael, "reckoned by almost universal opinion as the greatest of painters," lies buried in the Pantheon behind one of the altars. I went to Hadrian's

Tomb, now the Castle of St. Angelo, and on to St. Peter's. Before this great church-building there is a large open space containing an obelisk and two fountains, said to be the finest in the city, with a semi-circular colonnade on two sides containing two hundred and eighty-four columns in four rows, and on the top of the entablature there are ninety-six large statues. There are large figures on the top of the church, representing Christ and the apostles. The interior is magnificent. There are three aisles five hundred and seventy-five feet long, and the middle one is eighty-two feet wide. The beautifully ornamented ceiling is one hundred and forty-two feet high. In this building, which was completed three hundred and fifty years after it was begun, is the reputed tomb of the Apostle Peter, and many large marble statues. There are figures representing boy angels that are as large as a full-grown man. The Vatican is not far from St. Peter's, and I went up to see the Museum, but got there just as it was being closed for the day. I had a glimpse of the garden, and saw some of the Pope's carriages, which were fine indeed.

One of the most interesting places that I visited about Rome was the old underground cemetery called the Catacombs of St. Calixtus. The visitors go down a stairway with a guide, who leads them about the chambers, which are but dimly lighted by the small candles they carry. The passages, cut in the earth or soft rock, vary both in width and height, and have been explored in modern times to the aggregate length of six miles. Some of the bodies were placed in small recesses in the walls, but I saw none there as I went through, but there were two in marble coffins under glass. In one of the small chambers the party sang in some foreign language, probably Italian, and while I could not understand them, I thought the music sounded well. The Circus of Maxentius, fifteen hundred feet long and two hundred and sixty feet wide, is near the Catacombs, as is also the tomb of Caecilla Metella, which is said to have been erected more than nineteen hundred years ago. It is probably as much as two miles from the city walls, and I walked on a little way and could see other ruins still farther in the distance, but I turned back toward the hotel, and some time after sundown found myself walking along the banks of the yellow Tiber in the old city. Two days of sight-seeing had been well spent in and around the former capital of the world, and I was ready to go on to Naples the next day.

There is a saying, "See Naples and die," but I did not feel like expiring when I beheld it, although it is very beautifully located. The ruins of Pompeii, a few miles distant, had more interest for me than Naples. I went out there on the tenth of September, which I recollect as a very hot day. Pompeii, a kind of a summer resort for the Roman aristocracy, was founded 600 B.C. and destroyed by an eruption of Mt. Vesuvius in A.D. 79. It was covered with ashes from the volcano, and part of the population perished. The site of the city was lost, but was found after the lapse of centuries and the Italian

Government began the excavations in 1860. Some of the old stone-paved streets, showing the ruts made by chariot wheels that ceased to roll centuries ago, have been laid bare. Portions of the houses are still standing, and the stone drinking fountains along the streets are yet to be seen, as are also the stepping stones at the crossings, which are higher than the blocks used in paving. Some of the walls still contain very clear paintings, some of which are not at all commendable, and others are positively lewd. One picture represented a wild boar, a deer, a lion, a rabbit, some birds, and a female (almost nude) playing a harp. There was also a very clear picture of a bird and some cherries. At one place in the ruins I saw a well-executed picture of a chained dog in mosaic work. It is remarkable how well preserved some things are here. In the Museum are petrified bodies in the positions they occupied when sudden and unexpected destruction was poured upon them, well nigh two thousand years ago. Some appear to have died in great agony, but one has a peaceful position. Perhaps this victim was asleep when the death angel came. I saw the petrified remains of a dog wearing a collar and lying on his back, and a child on its face. One of the men, who may have been a military officer, seemed to have a rusty sword at his side. There were skeletons, both of human beings and of brutes, bronze vessels, and such articles as cakes and eggs from the kitchens of the old city.

Mt. Vesuvius is a very famous volcano, standing four thousand feet high, and has wrought a great deal of destruction. In the eruption of 472, it is related that its ashes were carried to Constantinople; in 1066, the lava flowed down to the sea; in 1631, eighteen thousand lives were lost; and in 1794 a stream of lava more than a thousand feet wide and fifteen feet high destroyed a town. From my hotel in Naples I had a fine view of the red light rising from the volcano the evening after I visited Pompeii.

Leaving Naples, I went to Brindisi, where I took ship for Patras in Greece. A day was spent in crossing Italy, two nights and a day were taken up with the voyage to Patras, and a good part of a day was occupied with the railroad trip from there to Athens, where the hotel men made more ado over me than I was accustomed to, but I got through all right and secured comfortable quarters at the New York Hotel, just across the street from the Parliament Building. From the little balcony at my window I could look out at the Acropolis. The principal places visited the first day were the Stadium, Mars' Hill, and the Acropolis.

Leaving the hotel and going through Constitution Square, up Philhellene Street, past the Russian and English churches, I came to the Zappeion, a modern building put up for Olympic exhibitions. The Arch of Hadrian, a peculiar old structure, twenty-three feet wide and about fifty-six feet high, stands near the Zappeion, and formerly marked the boundary between ancient Athens and the more modern part of the city. Passing through this arch, I soon came to what remains of the temple of the Olympian Jupiter, which was commenced long before the birth of Christ and finished by Hadrian about A.D. 140. Originally this temple, after that of Ephesus said to be the largest in the world, had three rows of eight columns each, on the eastern and western fronts, and a double row of one hundred columns on the northern and southern sides, and contained a statue of Jupiter, overlaid with gold and ivory. Its glory has long since departed, and only fifteen of the columns are now standing. A little farther on is the Stadium, with an arena over five hundred and eighty feet long, and one hundred and nine feet wide. It was originally constructed by the orator Lycurgus, about three hundred and fifty years before Christ, but was being rebuilt when I was there. The seats are on both sides and around the circular end of the arena, being made on the slope of the hill and covered with clean, white, Pentelic marble, making a beautiful sight.

On the way to Mars' Hill and the Acropolis I passed the monument of Lysicrates, the theater of Bacchus, and the Odeon. This first-mentioned theater is said to have been "the cradle of dramatic art," the masterpieces of Aeschylus, Sophocles, and others having been rendered there. The Odeon of Herod Atticus differed from other ancient theaters in that it was covered.

Mars' Hill is a great, oval-shaped mass of rock which probably would not be called a hill in America. The small end, which is the highest part of it, lies next to the Acropolis, and its summit is reached by going up a short flight of steps cut in the limestone, and well preserved, considering their age. The bluff on the opposite side from these steps is perhaps thirty or forty feet high and very rugged. The rock slopes toward the wide end, which is only a few feet above the ground. I estimate the greatest length of it to be about two hundred yards, and the greatest width one hundred and fifty yards, but accurate measurements might show these figures to be considerably at fault. I have spoken of the hill as a rock, and such it is—a great mass of hard limestone, whose irregular surface, almost devoid of soil, still shows where patches of it were dressed down, perhaps for ancient altars or idols. The Areopagus was a court, which in Paul's time had jurisdiction in cases pertaining to religion.

A vision called Paul into Macedonia, where Lydia was converted and Paul and Silas were imprisoned. In connection with their imprisonment, the conversion of the jailer of Philippi was brought about, after which the preachers went to Thessalonica, from whence Paul and Silas were sent to Berea. Jews from Thessalonica came down to Berea and stirred up the people, and the brethren sent Paul away, but Silas and Timothy were left behind. "They that conducted Paul, brought him as far as Athens," and then went back to Berea with a message to Silas and Timothy to come to him "with all speed." "Now while Paul waited for them at Athens, his spirit was provoked within him as he beheld the city full of idols." Being thus vexed, and having the gospel of Christ to preach, he reasoned with the Jews and devout people in the synagogue and every day in the marketplace with those he met there. He came in contact with philosophers of both the Epicurean and Stoic schools, and it was these philosophers who took him to the Areopagus, saying: "May we know what this new teaching is which is spoken by thee?"

The Athenians of those days were a pleasure-loving set of idolaters who gave themselves up to telling and hearing new things. Besides the many idols in the city, there were numerous temples and places of amusement. Within a few minutes' walk was the Stadium, capable of holding fifty thousand persons, and still nearer were the theater of Bacchus and the Odeon, capable of accommodating about thirty and six thousand people respectively. On the Acropolis, probably within shouting distance, stood some heathen temples, one of them anciently containing a colossal statue of Athene Parthenos, said to have been not less than thirty-nine feet high and covered with ivory and gold. In another direction and in plain sight stood, and still stands, the Theseum, a heathen temple at that time. Take all this into consideration, with the fact that Paul had already been talking with the people on religious subjects, and his great speech on Mars' Hill may be more impressive than ever before.

"Ye men of Athens, in all things I perceive that ye are very religious. For as I passed along and observed the objects of your worship, I found also an altar with this inscription, To an unknown God. What therefore ye worship in ignorance, this I set forth unto you. The God that made the world and all things therein, he being Lord of heaven and earth, dwelleth not in temples made with hands; neither is he served by men's hands as though he needed anything, seeing he himself giveth to all life, and breath, and all things; and he made of one every nation of men to dwell on all the face of the earth, having determined their appointed seasons, and the bounds of their habitation; that they should seek God, if haply they might feel after him and find him, though he is not far from each one of us; for in him we live, and move, and have our being; as certain even of your own poets have said, For we are also his offspring. Being then the offspring of God, we ought not to think the Godhead is like unto gold, or silver or stone, graven by art and device of man. The times of ignorance therefore God overlooked, but now he commandeth men that they should all everywhere repent: inasmuch as he hath appointed a day in the which he will judge the world in righteousness by the man whom he hath ordained; whereof he hath given assurance unto all men in that he hath raised him from the dead."

The Acropolis is a great mass of stone near Mars' Hill, but rising much higher and having a wall around its crest. At one time, it is said, the population of the city lived here, but later the city extended into the valley below and the

Acropolis became a fortress. About 400 B.C. the buildings were destroyed by the Persians, and those now standing there in ruins were erected by Pericles. The entrance, which is difficult to describe, is through a gateway and up marble stairs to the top, where there are large quantities of marble in columns, walls, and fragments. The two chief structures are the Parthenon and the Erectheum. The Parthenon is two hundred and eight feet long and one hundred and one feet wide, having a height of sixty-six feet. It is so large and situated in such a prominent place that it can be seen from all sides of the hill. In 1687 the Venetians while besieging Athens, threw a shell into it and wrecked a portion of it, but part of the walls and some of the fluted columns, which are more than six feet in diameter, are yet standing. This building is regarded as the most perfect model of Doric architecture in the world, and must have been very beautiful before its clear white marble was discolored by the hand of time and broken to pieces in cruel war. The Erectheum is a smaller temple, having a little porch with a flat roof supported by six columns in the form of female figures.

The Theseum, an old temple erected probably four hundred years before Christ, is the best preserved ruin of ancient Athens. It is a little over a hundred feet long, forty-five feet wide, and is surrounded by columns nearly nineteen feet high. The Hill of the Pynx lies across the road a short distance from the Theseum. At the lower side there is a wall of large stone blocks and above this a little distance is another wall cut in the solid rock, in the middle of which is a cube cut in the natural rock. This is probably the platform from which the speaker addressed the multitude that could assemble on the shelf or bench between the two walls.

Some of the principal modern buildings are the Hellenic Academy, the University, Library, Royal Palace, Parliament Building, various church buildings, hotels, and business houses. The University, founded in 1837, is rather plain in style, but is ornamented on the front after the manner of the ancients, with a number of paintings, representing Oratory, Mathematics, Geology, History, Philosophy, and other lines of study. At one end is a picture of Paul, at the other end, a representation of Prometheus. The museum is small and by no means as good as those to be seen in larger and wealthier countries. The Academy, finished in 1885, is near the University, and, although smaller than its neighbor, is more beautiful. On the opposite side of the University a fine new Library was being finished, and in the same street there is a new Roman Catholic church. I also saw two Greek Catholic church houses, but they did not seem to be so lavishly decorated within as the Roman church, but their high ceilings were both beautifully ornamented with small stars on a blue background. I entered a cemetery near one of these churches and enjoyed looking at the beautiful monuments and vaults. It is a common thing to find a representation of the deceased on the monument.

Some of these are full-length statues, others are carvings representing only the head. Lanterns, some of them lighted, are to be seen on many of the tombs. There are some fine specimens of the sculptor's art to be seen here, and the place will soon be even more beautiful, for a great deal of work was being done. In fact, the whole city of Athens seemed to be prosperous, from the amount of building that was being done.

The Parliament Building is not at all grand. The Royal Palace is larger and considerably finer. At the head of a stairway is a good picture of Prometheus tortured by an eagle. The visitor is shown the war room, a large hall with war scenes painted on the walls and old flags standing in the corners. The throne room and reception room are both open to visitors, as is also the ball room, which seemed to be more elaborately ornamented than the throne room. There is a little park of orange and other trees before the palace, also a small fountain with a marble basin. The highest point about the city is the Lycabettus, a steep rock rising nine hundred and nineteen feet above the level of the sea, and crowned with a church building. From its summit a splendid view of the city, the mountains, and the ocean may be obtained.

I spent five days in this city, the date of whose founding does not seem to be known. Pericles was one of the great men in the earlier history of the old city. He made a sacred enclosure of the Acropolis and placed there the masterpieces of Greece and other countries. The city is said to have had a population of three hundred thousand in his day, two-thirds of them being slaves. The names of Socrates, Demosthenes, and Lycurgus also belong to the list of great Athenians. In 1040 the Normans captured Piraeus, the seaport of Athens, and in 1455 the Turks, commanded by Omar, captured the city. The Acropolis was occupied by the Turks in 1826, but they surrendered the next year, and in 1839 Athens became the seat of government of the kingdom of Greece. With Athens, my sight-seeing on the continent ended. Other interesting and curious sights were seen besides those mentioned here. For instance, I had noticed a variety of fences. There were hedges, wire fences, fences of stone slabs set side by side, frail fences made of the stalks of some plant, and embryo fences of cactus growing along the railroad. In Italy, I saw many white oxen, a red ox being an exception that seems seldom to occur. I saw men hauling logs with oxen and a cart, the long timber being fastened beneath the axle of the cart and to the beam of the yoke. In Belgium, one may see horses worked three abreast and four tandem, and in Southern France they were shifting cars in one of the depots with a horse, and in France I also saw a man plowing with an ox and a horse hitched together. Now the time had come to enter the Turkish Empire, and owing to what I had previously heard of the Turk, I did not look forward to it with pleasure.

CHAPTER III.

ASIA MINOR AND SYRIA.

The Greek ship *Alexandros* left the harbor of Piraeus in the forenoon of Lord's day, September eighteenth, and anchored outside the breakwater at Smyrna, in Asia Minor, the next morning. The landing in Turkish territory was easily accomplished, and I was soon beyond the custom house, where my baggage and passport were examined, and settled down at the "Hotel d'Egypte," on the water front. This was the first time the passport had been called for on the journey. The population of Smyrna is a mixture of Turks, Greeks, Jews, Armenians, Italians, Americans, and Negroes. The English Government probably has a good sized representation, as it maintains its own postoffice. The city itself is the main sight. The only ruins I saw were those of an old castle on the hill back of the city. The reputed tomb of Polycarp is over this hill from Smyrna, between two cypress trees, but I do not know that I found the correct location. Near the place that I supposed to be the tomb is an aqueduct, a portion of it built of stone and a portion of metal. As I went on out in the country I entered a vineyard to get some grapes, not knowing how I would be received by the woman I saw there; but she was very kind-hearted, and when I made signs for some of the grapes, she at once pulled off some clusters and gave them to me. She also gave me a chair and brought some fresh water. More grapes were gathered and put in this cold water, so I had a fine time eating the fruit as I sat there in the shade watching a little boy playing about; but I could not converse with either of them on account of not knowing their language. On the way back to the city I stopped at the railway station to make inquiries about a trip to Ephesus.

Most of the streets in Smyrna are narrow and crooked, but there is one running along the water front that is rather attractive. On one side is the water, with the numerous vessels that are to be seen in this splendid harbor, and on the other side is a row of residences, hotels, and other buildings. The people turn out in great numbers at night and walk along this street, sometimes sitting down at the little tables that are set in the open air before places where different kinds of drinks are dispensed. Here they consume their drinks and watch the free performances that are given on an open stage adjoining the street and the grounds where they are seated. Perhaps the most peculiar thing about it all is the quiet and orderly behavior of this great crowd of people. While in this city I had occasion to go to the "Banque Imperiale Ottoman," and learned that it was open in the forenoon and afternoon, but closed awhile in the middle of the day. I saw a street barber plying his trade here one day. A vessel of water was put up under the customer's chin, and held there by keeping the chin down. The barber had his strop fastened to himself, and not to the chair or a wall, as we see it at home. Great quantities of oats were being brought down from the interior on camels. The sacks were let down on the pavement, and laborers were busy carrying them away. A poor carrier would walk up to a sack of grain and drop forward on his hands, with his head between them, and reaching down almost or altogether to the pavement. The sack of grain was then pulled over on his back, and he arose and carried it away. Some poor natives were busy sweeping the street and gathering up the grain that lost out of the sacks. There seems to be a large amount of trade carried on at this port. Several ships were in the harbor, and hundreds of camels were bringing in the grain. There are now many mosques and minarets in Smyrna, where there was once a church of God. (Revelation 2:8-11.)

On Wednesday, September twenty-first, I boarded a train on the Ottoman Railway for Ayassalouk, the nearest station to the ruins of Ephesus, a once magnificent city, "now an utter desolation, haunted by wild beasts." We left Smyrna at seven o'clock, and reached Ayassalouk, fifty miles distant, at half-past nine. The cars on this railway were entered from to side, as on European railroads, but this time the doors were locked after the passengers were in their compartments. Ayassalouk is a poor little village, with only a few good houses and a small population. At the back of the station are some old stone piers, that seem to have supported arches at an earlier date. On the top of the hill, as on many hilltops in this country, are the remains of an old castle. Below the castle are the ruins of what I supposed to be St. John's Church, built largely of marble, and once used as a mosque, but now inhabited by a large flock of martins.

I visited the site of Ephesus without the services of a guide, walking along the road which passes at some distance on the right. I continued my walk beyond the ruins, seeing some men plowing, and others caring for flocks of goats, which are very numerous in the East. When I turned back from the road, I passed a well, obtaining a drink by means of the rope and bucket that were there, and then I climbed a hill to the remains of a strong stone building of four rooms. The thick walls are several feet high, but all the upper part of the structure has been thrown down, and, strange to say, a good portion of the fallen rocks are in three of the rooms, which are almost filled. It is supposed that Paul made a journey after the close of his history in the book of Acts; that he passed through Troas, where he left a cloak and some books (2 Tim. 4:13); was arrested there, and probably sent to Ephesus for trial before the proconsul. Tradition has it that this ruined stone building is the place where he was lodged, and it is called St. Paul's Prison. From the top of its walls I could look away to the ruins of the city proper, about a mile distant, the theater being the most conspicuous object.

There are several attractions in Ephesus, where there was once a church of God—one of the "seven churches in Asia"—but the theater was the chief point of interest to me. It was cut out of the side of the hill, and its marble seats rested on the sloping sides of the excavation, while a building of some kind, a portion of which yet remains, was built across the open side at the front. I entered the inclosure, the outlines of which are still plainly discernible, and sat down on one of the old seats and ate my noonday meal. As I sat there, I thought of the scene that would greet my eyes if the centuries that have intervened since Paul was in Ephesus could be turned back. I thought I might see the seats filled with people looking down upon the apostle as he fought for his life; and while there I read his question: "If after the manner of men I fought with beasts at Ephesus, what doth it profit me" if the dead are not raised up? (I Cor. 15:32). I also read the letter which Jesus caused the aged Apostle John to write to the church at this place (Rev. 2:1-7), and Paul's epistle to the congregation that once existed in this idolatrous city of wealth and splendor. As I was leaving this spot, where I was so deeply impressed with thoughts of the great apostle to the Gentiles, I stopped and turned back to take a final look, when I thought of his language to Timothy, recorded in the first eight verses of the second epistle, and then I turned and read it. Perhaps I was not so deeply impressed at any other point on the whole journey as I was here. The grand old hero, who dared to enter the city which was "temple-keeper of the great Diana," this temple being one of the "Seven Wonders of the World," and boldly preach the gospel of Christ, realizing that the time of his departure was at hand, wrote: "I have fought the good fight, I have finished the course, I have kept the faith: Henceforth there is laid up for me the crown of righteousness, which the Lord, the righteous judge, shall give to me at that day; and not to me only, but also to all them that have loved his appearing." Meditating on the noble and lofty sentiment the apostle here expresses in connection with his solemn charge to the young evangelist, I have found my sentiments well expressed in Balaam's parable, where he says: "Let me die the death of the righteous, and let my last end be like his" (Num. 23:10).

Near the front of the theater, on the left as one comes out, is quite a space, which seems to have been excavated recently, and farther to the left excavations were being made when I was there. An ancient lamp, a fluted column, and a headless statue were among the articles taken out. The workmen were resting when I viewed this part of the ruins, and an old colored man gave me a drink of water. Beginning a little to the right of the theater, and extending for perhaps fifteen hundred or two thousand feet, is a marble-paved street, along which are strewn numerous bases, columns, and capitals, which once ornamented this portion of the great city; and to the right of this are the remains of some mighty structure of stone and brick. In some places, where the paving blocks have been taken up, a water course beneath is disclosed. While walking around in the ruins, I saw a fine marble sarcophagus, or coffin, ornamented with carvings of bulls' heads and heavy festoons of oak leaves.

J.S. Wood, an Englishman, worked parts of eleven years, from 1863 to 1874, in making excavations at Ephesus. Upwards of eighty thousand dollars were spent, about fifty-five thousand being used in a successful effort to find the remains of the Temple of Diana. I followed the directions of my guide-book, but may not have found the exact spot, as Brother McGarvey, who visited the place in 1879, speaks of the excavations being twenty feet deep. "Down in this pit," he says, "lie the broken columns of white marble and the foundation walls of the grandest temple ever erected on earth"; but I saw nothing like this.

When Paul had passed through Galatia and Phrygia, "establishing all the disciples," "having passed through the upper country," he came to Ephesus, and found "about twelve men" who had been baptized "into John's baptism," whom Paul baptized "into the name of the Lord Jesus." He then entered into the Jewish meeting place and reasoned boldly "concerning the kingdom of God." Some of the hardened and disobedient spoke "evil of the Way," so Paul withdrew from them and reasoned "daily in the school of Tyrannus. And this continued for the space of two years; so that all they that dwelt in Asia heard the word of the Lord, both Jews and Greeks." The Lord wrought special miracles by Paul, so that the sick were healed when handkerchiefs or aprons were borne from him to them. Here some of the strolling Jews "took upon them to name over them that had the evil spirits the name of the Lord Jesus, saying, I adjure you by Jesus, whom Paul preacheth." When two of the sons of Sceva undertook to do this, the man possessed of the evil spirit "leaped on them and mastered both of them, and prevailed against them, so that they fled out of the house naked and wounded." There were stirring times in Ephesus in those days. Fear fell upon the people, "and the name of the Lord Jesus was magnified." Many of the believers "came confessing, and declaring their deeds. And not a few of them that practiced magical arts brought their books together and burned them in the sight of all; and they counted the price of them, and found it fifty thousand pieces of silver." "So mightily grew the word of the Lord and prevailed."

"And about that time there arose no small stir concerning the Way. For a certain man named Demetrius, a silversmith who made silver shrines of Diana, brought no little business unto the craftsmen; whom he gathered together, with the workmen of like occupation, and said, Sirs, ye know that by this business we have our wealth. And ye see and hear that not alone at Ephesus, but almost throughout all Asia, this Paul hath persuaded and turned away much people, saying that they are no gods that are made with hands: and not only is there danger that our trade come into disrepute, but also that the temple of the great goddess Diana be made of no account, and that she should even be deposed from her magnificence, whom all Asia and the world worshipeth. And when they heard this they were filled with wrath, and cried out, saying, Great is Diana of the Ephesians. And the city was filled with the confusion: and they rushed with one accord into the theater, having seized Gaius and Aristarchus, men of Macedonia, Paul's companions in travel. And when Paul was minded to enter in unto the people, the disciples suffered him not. And certain also of the Asiarchs, being his friends, sent unto him and besought him not to adventure himself into the theater. Some therefore cried one thing, and some another: for the assembly was in confusion; and the more part knew not wherefore they were come together. And they brought Alexander out of the multitude, the Jews putting him forward. And Alexander beckoned with the hand and would have made a defense unto the people. But when they perceived that he was a Jew, all with one voice about the space of two hours cried out, Great is Diana of the Ephesians. And when the town clerk had quieted the multitude, he saith, Ye men of Ephesus, what man is there who knoweth not that the city of the Ephesians is temple-keeper of the great Diana, and of the image which fell down from Jupiter? Seeing then that these things can not be gainsaid, ye ought to be quiet, and to do nothing rash. For ye have brought hither these men, who are neither robbers of temples nor blasphemers of our goddess. If therefore Demetrius, and the craftsmen that are with him, have a matter against any man, the courts are open, and there are proconsuls: let them accuse one another. But if ye seek anything about other matters, it shall be settled in the regular assembly. For indeed we are in danger to be accused concerning this day's riot, there being no cause for it: and as touching it we shall not be able to give an account of this concourse. And when he had thus spoken, he dismissed the assembly" (Acts 19:23-41).

As I was leaving the ruins, I stopped, sat down in sight of the spot where I supposed the temple stood, and read the speech of Demetrius, and thought his fears were well founded. Their trade has come into disrepute, "the temple of the great goddess" has been "made of no account," and "she whom Asia and all the world" worshiped has been "deposed from her magnificence." Portions of the temple are now on exhibition in the British Museum, in London, and portions have been carried to different other cities to adorn buildings inferior to the one in which they were originally used. "From the temple to the more southern of the two eastern gates of the city," says McGarvey, "are traces of a paved street nearly a mile in length, along the side of which was a continuous colonnade, with the marble coffins of the city's illustrious dead occupying the spaces between the columns. The processions of worshipers, as they marched out of the city to the temple, passed by this row of coffins, the inscriptions on which were constantly proclaiming the noble deeds of the mighty dead." The canal and artificial harbor, which enabled the ships of the world to reach the gates of the city, have disappeared under the weight of the hand of time. In some places the ground is literally covered with small stones, and even in the theater, weeds, grass and bushes grow undisturbed. How complete the desolation!

Before leaving Ayassalouk on the afternoon train, I bought some grapes of a man who weighed them to me with a pair of balances, putting the fruit on one pan and a stone on the other; but I didn't object to his scales, for he gave me a good supply, and I went back and got some more. I also bought some bread to eat with the grapes, and one of the numerous priests of these Eastern countries gave me some other fruit on the train. I was abroad in the fruit season, and I enjoyed it very much. I had several kinds, including the orange, lemon, grapes, pomegranates, figs, olives, and dates. Perhaps I had nothing finer than the large, sweet grapes of Greece. The next day after the trip to Ephesus, I boarded the *Princess Eugenia*, a Russian ship, for Beyrout, in Syria. Soon after leaving Smyrna the ship stopped at a port of disinfection. The small boats were lowered, and the third-class passengers were carried to the disinfecting establishment, where their clothes were heated in a steam oven, while they received a warm shower bath without expense to themselves. A nicely dressed young German shook his head afterwards, as though he did not like such treatment; but it was not specially disagreeable, and there was no use to complain.

That evening, the twenty-second of September, we sailed into a harbor on the island of Chios, the birth-place of the philosopher Pythagoras. It is an island twenty-seven miles long, lying near the mainland. The next morning we passed Cos and Rhodes. On this last mentioned island once stood the famous Colossus, which was thrown down by an earthquake in 224 B.C. The island of Patmos, to which John was banished, and upon which he wrote the Revelation, was passed in the night before we reached Cos. It is a rocky, barren patch of land, about twenty miles in circumference, lying twenty-four miles from the coast of Asia Minor. On the twenty-fourth the *Princess Eugenia* passed the southwestern end of the island of Cyprus. In response to a question, one of the seamen answered me: "Yes, that's Kiprus." I was sailing over the same waters Paul crossed on his third missionary tour on the way from Assos to Tyre. He "came over against Chios," "came with a straight course unto Cos, and the next day unto Rhodes," and when he "had come in sight of Cyprus, leaving it on the left hand (he) sailed unto Syria and landed at Tyre" (Acts 20:15 and 21:1-3).

On the evening of Lord's day, September twenty-fifth, the ship passed Tripoli, on the Syrian coast, and dropped down to Beyrout, where I stopped at the "Hotel Mont Sion," with the waves of the Mediterranean washing against the foundation walls. At seven o'clock the next morning I boarded the train for Damascus, ninety-one miles distant, and we were soon climbing the western slope of the Lebanon Mountains by a cog railway. When we were part way up, the engine was taken back and hitched to the rear end of the train. After we were hauled along that way awhile, it was changed back to the front end again. In these mountains are vineyards and groves of figs, olives, and mulberry trees, but most of the ground was dry and brown, as I had seen it in Southern Italy, Greece, and Asia Minor. Beyond the mountains is a beautiful plain, which we entered about noon, and when it was crossed, we came to the Anti-Lebanon Mountains, and reached the old city in the evening. Damascus, with its mixed population of Moslems, Greeks, Syrians, Armenians, Jews, and others, is the largest city in Syria, and it has probably been continuously inhabited longer than any other city on earth. Away back in the fourteenth chapter of Genesis we read of Abraham's victory over the enemies who had taken Lot away, whom Abraham pursued "unto Hobah, which is on the left of Damascus," and in the next chapter we read of "Eliezer of Damascus," who Abraham thought would be the possessor of his house. Rezon "reigned in Damascus, and he was an adversary to Israel all the days of Solomon" (1 Kings 11:23-25). Elisha went to Damascus when Ben-Hadad was sick (2 Kings 8:7-15); Jeroboam recovered the city, which had belonged to Judah (2 Kings 14:28); and Jeremiah prophesied of the city (Jeremiah 49:23-27). It was probably the home of Naaman, the Syrian leper, and here Paul was baptized into Christ.

For a long time the Arabs have considered Damascus as "an earthly reflection of Paradise," but an American or European would consider a place no better than it is as being far from the Paradise of Divine making. But it is not entirely without reason that these people have such a lofty conception of the old city. The Koran describes Paradise as a place of trees and streams of water, and Damascus is briefly described in those words. There are many public drinking fountains in the city, and owing to the abundance of water, there are many trees. The river Abana, one of the "rivers of Damascus" (2 Kings 5:12), flows through the city, but the most of its water is diverted by artificial channels. I had some difficulty in finding the American Consular Agent, and it is no wonder, for the place is not the most prominent in Damascus by a good deal, and the escutcheon marking it as the place where the American Government is represented is not on the street, but over a door in a kind of porch. The Agent was not in, so I retraced my steps to the French consulate, which is near by. I was kindly received by a gentleman who could speak English, and after we had had a good, cool drink of lemonade, he went with me to the "Hotel d'Astre d'Orient," in the "street which is called Straight." The next morning I found the American Agent in his office. Then I went to the postoffice, and after being taken upstairs and brought back downstairs, I was led up to a little case on the wall, which was unlocked in order that I might look through the bunch of letters it contained addressed in English, and I was made glad by receiving an epistle from the little woman who has since taken my name upon her for life. After reading my letter, I went out and walked up the mountain side far enough to get a bird's-eye view of the city, and it was a fine sight the rich growth of green trees presented in contrast with the brown earth all around. Returning to the city, I walked about the streets, devoting some of my time to the bazaars, or little stores, in which a great variety of goods are offered for sale. I also saw several kinds of work, such as weaving, wood-turning and blacksmithing, being carried on. The lathes used for turning wood are very simple, and are operated by a bow held in the workman's right hand, while the chisel is held in his left hand and steadied by the toes on one or the other of his feet. It is a rather slow process, but they can turn out good work. One gentleman, who was running a lathe of this kind, motioned for me to come up and sit by his side on a low stool. I accepted his invitation, and he at once offered me a cigarette, which I could not accept. A little later he called for a small cup of coffee, which I also declined, but he took no offense. "The street which is called Straight" is not as straight as might be supposed from its name, but there is probably enough difference between its course and that of others to justify the name.

When Paul was stricken with blindness on his way here (Acts 9:1-30), he was directed to enter the city, where he would be told all things that were appointed for him to do. He obeyed the voice from heaven, and reached the house of Judas in Straight Street. When I reached the traditional site of the house of Ananias, in the eastern part of the city, near the gate at the end of Straight Street, I found a good-natured woman sitting on the pavement just inside the door opening from the street to what would be called a yard in America. The "house" has been converted into a small church, belonging to the Catholics, and it is entirely below the surface. I went down the stairs, and found a small chamber with an arched ceiling and two altars. I also went out and visited the old gateway at the end of the street. The masonry is about thirteen feet thick, and it may be that here Paul, deprived of his sight, and earnestly desiring to do the will of the Lord, entered the city so long ago. I then viewed a section of the wall from the outside. The lower part is ancient, but the upper part is modern, and the portion that I saw was in a dilapidated condition. "In Damascus," Paul wrote to the Corinthians, "the governor, under Aretas the king, guarded the city of the Damascenes in order to take me: and through a window was I let down in a basket by the wall, and escaped his hands" (2 Cor. 11:32,33). In some places there are houses so built in connection with the wall that it would not be a very difficult thing to lower a man from one of the windows to the ground outside the city.

Mention has already been made of the Arab's opinion of Damascus, and now I wish to tell how it appeared through my spectacles. The view from the distance is very pleasing, but when one comes inside the wall and begins to walk about the streets, the scene changes. The outside of the buildings is not beautiful. The streets are narrow, crooked, and usually very dirty; in some cases they are filthy. It seems that all kinds of rubbish are thrown into the streets, and the dogs are scavengers. Perhaps no other city has so many dogs. At one place up along the Abana, now called the Barada, I counted twenty-three of these animals, and a few steps brought me in sight of five more; but there is some filth that even Damascus dogs will not clean up. Some of the streets are roughly paved with stone, but in the best business portion of the city that I saw there was no pavement and no sidewalk—it was all street from one wall to the other. I saw a man sprinkling one of the streets with water carried in the skin of some animal, perhaps a goat. When I came out of the postoffice, a camel was lying on the pavement, and in another part of the city I saw a soldier riding his horse on the sidewalk. Down in "the street which is called Straight" a full-grown man was going along as naked as when he was born. Perhaps he was insane, but we do not even allow insane men to walk the streets that way in this country. Carriages are used for conveying passengers, but freight is usually moved on the backs of horses, camels, donkeys, or men. Some wagons and carts are to be seen, but they are not numerous. It is remarkable what loads are piled upon the donkeys, probably the commonest beasts of burden in Damascus. Sometimes the poor little creatures are almost hidden from view by the heavy burdens they are required to bear, which may consist of grapes to be sold, or rubbish to be carried out of the city. Sometimes they are ridden by as many as three people at once. If the gospel were to get a firm hold on these people, the donkeys would fare better.

About 333 B.C., Damascus came under the control of Alexander the Great. Antiochus Dionysius reigned there three years, but was succeeded by Aretas of Arabia in 85 B.C. Under Trajan it became a Roman provincial city. The Mongols took it in 1260, and the Tartars plundered it in 1300. An enemy marched against it in 1399, but the citizens purchased immunity from plunder by paying a "sum of a million pieces of gold." In 1516, when Selim, the Turkish Sultan, marched in, it became one of the provincial capitals of the Turkish Empire, and so continues. There was a very serious massacre here in 1860. All the consulates, except the British and Prussian, were burned, and the entire Christian quarter was turned into ruins. In the two consulates that were spared many lives were preserved, but it is said that "no fewer than six thousand unoffending Christians ... were thus murdered in Damascus alone," and "the whole number of the Christians who perished in these days of terror is estimated at fourteen thousand." A number of the leaders were afterward beheaded, and a French force, numbering ten thousand, was sent into the country. The Mohammedans have about two hundred mosques and colleges in this city, which was once far advanced in civilization.

I left Damascus and returned toward the coast to Rayak, where I took the train on a branch line for Baalbec, the Syrian city of the sun, a place having no Biblical history, but being of interest on account of the great stones to be seen there. No record has been preserved as to the origin of the city, but coins of the first century of the Christian era show that it was then a Roman colony. It is situated in the valley of the Litany, at an elevation of two thousand eight hundred and forty feet above the sea. The chief ruins are in a low part of the valley by the side of the present town, and are surrounded by gardens. Within the inclosing wall are the remains of the temple of Jupiter and the temple of the sun. The hand of time and the hand of man have each had a share in despoiling these ruins, but they still speak with eloquence of their grandeur at an earlier date. The wall is so low on the north that it is supposed to have been left unfinished. Here are nine stones, each said to be thirty feet long, ten feet thick and thirteen feet high, and they are closely joined together without the use of mortar. Just around the corner are three others still larger, and built in the wall about twenty feet above the foundation. Their lengths are given as follows: sixty-three feet; sixty-three feet and eight inches; and sixty-four feet. They are thirteen feet high and about ten feet thick. Some may be interested in knowing how such large building blocks were moved. McGarvey says: "It is explained by the carved slabs found in the temple of Nineveh, on which are sculptured representations of the entire process. The great rock was placed on trucks by means of levers, a large number of strong ropes were tied to the truck, a smooth track of heavy timbers was laid, and men in sufficient number to move the mass were hitched to the ropes." Some of the smaller stones have holes cut in them, as if for bars, levers, or something of that kind, but the faces of these big blocks are smooth. "A man must visit the spot, ride round the exterior, walk among the ruins, sit down here and there to gaze upon its more impressive features, see the whole by sunlight, by twilight, and by moonlight, and allow his mind leisurely to rebuild it and re-people it, ere he can comprehend it."—*McGarvey.*

There were some of the native girls out by the ruins who tried to sell me some of their needle work, but I was not disposed to buy. One of them attempted to make a sale by saying something like this: "You're very nice, Mister; please buy one." I told her there was a little girl in America who thought that, too, and went on. There is a rock in the quarry at Baalbec that is larger than any of those in the ruins, although it was never entirely cut out, the length of which is sixty-eight feet, and the width varies from about thirteen feet at one end to seventeen feet at the other. It is about fourteen feet thick, and the estimated weight is fifteen hundred tons. Some of the stones in a ruined building, once a tomb, standing on the hill above the town, give forth a metallic ring when struck. Farther on is a small cemetery, in which some of the headstones and footstones are as much as nine feet apart. If the people buried there were that long, surely "there were giants in the land in those days." I went down on the opposite side of the hill from the tomb and entered a vineyard, where an old man treated me with kindness and respect. The modern town is poorly built of small stones and mud, but there are some good buildings of dressed stone, among which I may mention the British Syrian School and the Grand New Hotel. I staid at another hotel, where I found one of those pre-occupied beds which travelers in the East so often find. About midnight, after I had killed several of the little pests, I got up and shaved by candle-light, for I wasn't sleepy, and there was no use to waste the time.

Leaving Baalbec, I went down to Rayak and on to Beyrout again. This old city is said to have been entirely destroyed in the second century before Christ. It was once a Roman possession, and gladiatorial combats were held there by Titus after the destruction of Jerusalem. An earthquake destroyed it in 529, and the British bombarded it in 1840. The population is a great mixture of Turks, Orthodox Greeks, United Greeks, Jews, Latins, Maronites, Protestants, Syrians, Armenians, Druses, and others. A great many ships call here, as this is the most important commercial city in Syria. The numerous exports consist of silk, olive oil, cotton, raisins, licorice, figs, soap, sponges, cattle, and goats. Timber, coffee, rice, and manufactured goods are imported. At one time Arabic was the commonest language, and Italian came next, but now, while Arabic holds first place, French comes second. The British, Austrians, Russians, and perhaps the French, maintain their own postoffices. Considerable efforts are being made by American, British, and other missionary institutions to better the condition of the natives. The American Mission, conducted by the Presbyterians, has been in operation more than seventy years. A few years ago they had one hundred and forty-three schools and more than seven thousand pupils. The Church of Scotland has a mission for the Jews. The British Syrian Mission was established in 1864.

Beyrout has comparatively little of interest for the traveler. I walked out to the public garden one morning and found it closed, but I do not think I missed much. As I went along from place to place, I had opportunity to see the weavers, wood-turners, and marble-cutters at their work. I stopped at a small candy factory, equipped with what seemed to be good machinery for that kind of work. One day I watched some camels get up after their burdens of lumber had been tied on. They kept up a peculiar distressing noise while they were being loaded, but got up promptly when the time came. When a camel lies down, his legs fold up something like a carpenter's rule, and when he gets up, he first straightens out one joint of the fore legs, then all of the hind legs, and finally, when the fore legs come straight, he is standing away up in the air. The extensive buildings of the American College were visited, also the American Press, the missionary headquarters of Presbyterians in America. On the third of October the Khedivial steamer *Assouan* came along, and I embarked for Haifa, in Galilee.

CHAPTER IV.

A FEW DAYS IN GALILEE.

Years ago, when I first began to think of making the trip I am now describing, I had no thought of the many interesting places that I could easily and cheaply visit on my way to Palestine. I did not then think of what has been described on the foregoing pages. Now I have come to the place where I am to tell my readers the story of my travels in the Land of Promise, and I want to make it as interesting and instructive as possible. It is important to have a knowledge of the geography of all the lands mentioned, but it is especially important to know the location of the various places referred to in Palestine. These pages will be more profitable if the reader will make frequent reference to maps of the land, that he may understand the location of the different places visited. I shall first describe my trip across the province of Galilee, and take up my sight-seeing in Judaea in other chapters.

The ancient Phoenician cities of Tyre and Sidon were on the coast between Beyrout and Haifa, where I entered Galilee on the fourth of October, but we passed these places in the night. Haifa, situated at the base of Mount Carmel, has no Biblical history, but is one of the two places along the coast of Palestine where ships stop, Jaffa being the other. Mount Carmel is fourteen miles long, and varies in height from five hundred and fifty-six feet at the end next to the sea to eighteen hundred and ten feet at a point twelve miles inland. There is a monastery on the end next to the Mediterranean, which I reached after a dusty walk along the excellent carriage road leading up from Haifa. After I rested awhile, reading my Bible and guide-book, I walked out to the point where the sea on three sides, the beautiful little plain at the base of the mountain, Haifa, and Acre across the bay, all made up one of the prettiest views of the whole trip. Owing to its proximity to the sea and the heavy dews, Carmel was not so dry and brown as much of the country I had seen before.

By the direction of Elijah, Ahab gathered the prophets of Baal, numbering four hundred and fifty, and the prophets of the Asherah, four hundred more, at some point on this mountain, probably at the eastern end, passed on my way over to Nazareth later in the day. "And Elijah came near unto all the people, and said, How long go ye limping between the two sides? If Jehovah be God, follow him; but if Baal, then follow him" (1 Kings 18:21). He then proposed that two sacrifices be laid on the wood, with no fire under them; that the false prophets should call on their god, and he would call on Jehovah. The God that answered by fire was to be God. "All the people answered and said, It is well spoken." The prophets of Baal called upon him from morning till noon, saying, "O Baal, hear us. But there was no voice, nor any that answered. And they leaped about the altar that was made. And it came to pass at noon that Elijah mocked them, and said, Cry aloud; for he is a god: either he is musing, or he is gone aside, or he is on a journey, or peradventure he sleepeth and must be awaked. And they cried aloud, and cut themselves after their manner with knives and lances, till the blood gushed out upon them. And it was so, when midday was past, that they prophesied until the time of the offering of the evening oblation; but there was neither voice, nor any to answer, nor any that regarded." The sincerity, earnestness, and perseverance of these people are commendable, but they were *wrong*. Sincerity, although a most desirable trait, can not change a wrong act into acceptable service to God, nor can earnestness and perseverance make such a change. It is necessary both to be honest and to do the will of our heavenly Father. After water had been poured over the other sacrifice till it ran down and filled the trench around the altar, Elijah called on Jehovah, and in response to his petition "the fire of Jehovah fell, and consumed the burnt offering, and the wood, and the stones, and the dust, and licked up the water that was in the trench." Elijah then took the false prophets down to the brook Kishon, at the base of the mountain, and killed them. Acre is the Acco of the Old Testament, and lies around the bay, twelve mile from Haifa. It is said that the Phoenicians obtained the dye called Tyrian purple there, and that shells of the fish that yielded it are yet to be found along the beach. Napoleon besieged the place in 1799, and used a monastery, since destroyed, on Mount Carmel for a hospital. After his retreat, Mohammedans killed the sick and wounded soldiers who had been left behind, and they were buried near the monastery. Acre was called Ptolemais in apostolic times, and Paul spent a day with the brethren there as he was on his way down the coast from Tyre to Jerusalem. (Acts 21:7.)

About noon I entered a carriage for Nazareth, in which there were four other passengers: a lady connected with the English Orphanage in Nazareth, and three boys going there to attend the Russian school. About two miles from Haifa we crossed the dry bed of the Kishon, as this stream, like many others in Palestine, only flows in the wet season. Our course led along the base of Carmel to the southeast, and the supposed place of Elijah's sacrifice was pointed out. Afterwards Mount Gilboa, where Saul and Jonathan were slain, came in sight, and later we saw Little Hermon with Nain upon it, Endor below it on one side, and Jezreel not far away in another direction. We saw a good portion of the Plain of Esdraelon, and Mount Tabor was in sight before we entered Nazareth, which lies on the slope of a hill and comes suddenly into view.

Nazareth is not mentioned in the Old Testament, and the references to it in the New Testament are not numerous. When Joseph returned from Egypt in the reign of Archelaus, the son of Herod, he was afraid to go into Judaea, "and being warned of God in a dream, he withdrew into the parts of Galilee, and came and dwelt in a city called Nazareth; that it might be fulfilled which was spoken by the prophet, that he should be called a Nazarene" (Matt. 2:19-23). I do not know the age of Jesus when Joseph and Mary came with him to Nazareth, but "his parents went every year to Jerusalem at the feast of the passover"; and we are told that the child was twelve years old at the time his parents missed him as they were returning from the feast, and later found him in the temple hearing the teachers and asking them questions. In this connection we are told that "he went down with them and came to Nazareth; and he was subject unto them" (Luke 2:51). Luke also informs us that Jesus, "when he began to teach, was about thirty years of age" (Luke 3:23). Thus we have a period of eighteen years between the incident in the temple and the beginning of his public ministry, in which Jesus resided in Nazareth. The greater part of his earth life was spent in this Galilean city, where he was subject unto his parents. It is a blessed thing that so much can be said of our Savior in so few words. It is highly commendable that children be subject unto their parents, who love them dearly, and who know best what is for their health, happiness, and future good.

After his baptism and temptation in the wilderness, "Jesus returned in the power of the spirit into Galilee, ... and he came to Nazareth, where he had been brought up: and he entered, as his custom was, into the synagogue on the Sabbath day and stood up to read." When the roll of the Scriptures was handed to him, he read from the opening verses of the sixty-first chapter of Isaiah, then "he closed the book, and gave it back to the attendant, and sat down: and the eyes of all in the synagogue were fastened on him" as he told them: "To-day hath this scripture been fulfilled in your ears," and although they "wondered at the words of grace which proceeded out of his mouth," they were not willing to accept his teaching, and as he continued to speak, "they were all filled with wrath, ... and they rose up, and cast him forth out of the city, and led him unto the brow of the hill whereon their city was built, that they might throw him down headlong. But he, passing through the midst of them, went his way. And he came down to Capernaum, a city of Galilee" (Luke 4:14-31).

Having made arrangements for a carriage the evening I arrived in Nazareth, before daylight the next morning I started to drive to Tiberias, on the Sea of Galilee. When I went down stairs, at about half-past three o'clock, I found a covered rig with two seats, and three horses hitched to it side by side. I filed no objection to the size of the carriage, nor to the manner in which the horses were hitched. As the driver could not speak English and the passenger could not speak Arabic, there was no conversation on the way. As we drove out of Nazareth, I observed a large number of women at the Virgin's Fountain, filling their jars with water. At a distance of a little more than three miles we passed through Kefr Kenna, the "Cana of Galilee," where Jesus performed his first miracle. (John 2:1-11.) The road to Tiberias is not all smooth, but is better than might be supposed. With three horses and a light load, we were able to move along in the cool of the morning at a lively gait, passing a camel train, an occasional village, olive orchard, or mulberry grove. After a while the light of the moon grew pale, and about six o'clock the great round sun came above the horizon in front of us, and it was not long until a beautiful sheet of water six miles long—the Sea of Galilee—came suddenly into view. We rolled along the winding curves of the carriage road, down the slope of the hill, and through a gateway in the old wall, to Tiberias, on the west shore of "Blue Galilee."

According to Josephus, Herod Antipas began to build a new capital city about sixteen years before the birth of Jesus, and completed it in A.D. 22. He named this new city Tiberias, in honor of the emperor, but it does not appear to have been a popular place with the Jews, and but little is said of it in the New Testament (John 21:1), yet it was not an insignificant place. The Sanhedrin was transferred from Sepphoris, the old capital, to the new city, and here the school of the Talmud was developed against the gospel system. The ancient traditional law, called the "Mishna," is said to have been published here in A.D. 200, and the Palestinian Gemara (the so-called Jerusalem Talmud) came into existence at this place more than a century later. The Tiberian pointing of the Hebrew Bible began here. The present population is largely composed of Jews, about two-thirds of the inhabitants being descendants of Abraham. They wear large black hats or fur caps, and leave a long lock of hair hanging down in front of each ear. There is little in Tiberias to interest the traveler who has seen the ruins of Rome, Athens and Ephesus. The seashore bounds it on one side and an old stone wall runs along at the other side. I walked past some of the bazaars, and saw the mosque and ruined castle. About a mile down the shore are the hot springs, which, for many centuries, have been thought to possess medicinal properties. I tried the temperature of one of the springs, and found it too hot to be comfortable to my hand. As I returned to Tiberias, I had a good, cool bath in the sea, which is called by a variety of names, as "the sea of Tiberias," "sea of Galilee," "sea of Genessaret," and "sea of Chinnereth." It is a small lake, thirteen miles long, lying six hundred and eighty-two feet below the level of the Mediterranean. The depth is given as varying from one hundred and thirty to one hundred and sixty-five feet. It is really "Blue Galilee," and the sight of it is an agreeable change to the eye after one has been traveling the dry, dusty roads leading through a country almost destitute of green vegetation. In the spring, when the grass is growing and the flowers are in bloom, the highlands rising around the sea must be very beautiful.

Several places mentioned in the New Testament were situated along the Sea of Galilee, but they have fallen into ruin—in some cases into utter ruin. One of these was Bethsaida, where Jesus gave sight to a blind man (Mark 8:22-26), and fed a multitude of about five thousand. (Luke 9:10-17.) It was also the home of Philip, Andrew, and Peter. (John 1:44.) It is thought by some that James and John also came from this place. On the northwestern shore was Chorazin, situated in the neighborhood of Bethsaida; also Capernaum, once the home of Jesus; and Magdala, the name of which "has been immortalized in every language of Christendom as denoting the birth-place of Mary Magdalene, or better, Mary of Magdala." Safed is a large place on a mountain above the sea in sight of the Nazareth road, and was occupied by the French in 1799. It is said that the Jews have a tradition that the Messiah will come from this place. On the way back to Nazareth the driver stopped at the spring of Kefr Kenna and watered his horses and rested them awhile. Hundreds of goats, calves, and other stock were being watered, and I saw an old stone coffin being used for a watering trough.

After another night in Nazareth, I was ready to go out to Mount Tabor. For this trip I had engaged a horse to ride and a man to go along and show me where to ride it, for we did not follow a regular road, if, indeed, there is any such a thing leading to this historic place, which is about six miles from Nazareth. It was only a little past four o'clock in the morning when we started, and the flat top of the mountain, two thousand and eighteen feet above sea level, was reached at an early hour. Mount Tabor is a well-shaped cone, with a good road for horseback riding leading up its side. There is some evidence that there was a city here more than two hundred years before Christ. Josephus fortified it in his day, and part of the old wall still remains. According to a tradition, contradicted by the conclusion of modern scholars, this is the mount of transfiguration. By the end of the sixth century three churches had been erected on the summit to commemorate the three tabernacles which Peter proposed to build (Matt. 17:1-8), and now the Greek and Roman Catholics have each a monastery only a short distance apart, separated by a stone wall or fence. The extensive view from the top is very fine, including a section of Galilee from the Mediterranean to the sea of Tiberias.

In the Book of Judges we read that Israel was delivered into the hands of the Canaanites, and was sorely oppressed for twenty years. The prophetess Deborah sent for Barak, and instructed him with a message from God to the end that he should take "ten thousand men of the children of Naphtali and of the children of Zebulun" unto Mount Tabor. This he did, and Sisera assembled his nine hundred chariots "from Harosheth of the Gentiles unto the river Kishon. So Barak went down from Mount Tabor and ten thousand men after him. ... Howbeit, Sisera fled away on his feet to the tent of Jael, the wife of Heber, the Kenite," and she drove a tent-pin through his temples while he was lying asleep, (Judges 4:1-23.) The song of Deborah and Barak, beginning with the words, "For that the leaders took the lead in Israel, for that the people offered themselves willingly, bless ye Jehovah," is recorded in the fifth chapter of Judges.

I was back in Nazareth by ten o'clock, and spent some hours looking around the city where the angel Gabriel announced to Mary the words: "Hail, thou that art highly favored, the Lord is with thee" (Luke 1:28). These hours, with what time I had already spent here, enabled me to see several places of interest. Tradition points out many places connected with the lives of Joseph and Mary, but tradition is not always reliable, for it sometimes happens that the Greeks and the Romans each have a different location for the same event. This is true with regard to the point where the angry people were about to throw Jesus over "the brow of the hill" (Luke 4:29). I saw no place that struck me as being the one referred to in the Scriptures, and in reply to an inquiry, a lady at the English Orphanage, who has spent twenty years in Nazareth, said she thought it was some place on that side of the town, but the contour of the hill had probably changed. She also mentioned that the relics taken out in excavations were all found on that side, indicating that the old city had been built there. When Brother McGarvey visited Palestine, he found two places that corresponded somewhat with Luke's reference to the place. Concerning one of them he wrote: "I am entirely satisfied that here is where the awful attempt was made." I was shown the "place of annunciation" in the Latin monastery. On the top of a column stands the figure of a female, probably representing the Virgin, and a bit of ruin that is said to date back to the time of Constantine is pointed out. Here, I was told, stood the first church building erected in Nazareth. One of the "brothers" took the key and went around to a building supposed to stand on the site of Joseph's carpenter shop. It is a small chapel, built about 1858 over the ruins of some older structure. In the floor of marble or stone there are two wooden trapdoors, which are raised to show the ruins below. Over the altar in the end opposite the door is a picture to represent the holy family, and there are some other pictures in different parts of the little chapel. From here I went to the Virgin's Fountain. If it be true that this is the only spring in Nazareth, then I have no doubt that I was near the spot frequently visited by the Nazarene maid who became the mother of our Lord. I say near the spot, for the masonry where the spring discharges is about a hundred yards from the fountain, which is now beneath the floor of a convent. The water flows out through the wall by two stone spouts, and here the women were crowded around, filling their vessels or waiting for their turn. The flow was not very strong, and this helps to explain why so many women were there before daylight the morning I went to Tiberias. I saw one woman, who was unable to get her vessel under the stream of one of the spouts, drawing down a part of the water by sticking a leaf against the end of the spout. I also visited some of the bazaars and went to the Orphanage. This missionary institution is nicely situated in a prominent place well up on the hill, and is managed entirely by women, but a servant is kept to do outside work. They treated me very kindly, showing me about the building, and when the girls came in to supper they sang "the Nazareth Hymn" for me.

One of the occupations of the people here is manufacturing a knife with goat horn handles that is commonly seen in Palestine. Many of the women go about the streets with their dresses open like a man's shirt when unbuttoned, exposing their breasts in an unbecoming manner. The same is true of many women in Jerusalem. About one-third of the mixed population are Jews; the other two-thirds are Mohammedans and professing Christians, made up of Orthodox Greeks, United Greeks, Roman Catholics, Maronites (a branch of the Greek Church), and Protestants. I went back to Haifa and spent a night. The next morning I boarded the Austrian ship *Juno* for Jaffa. When I first landed here I had trouble with the boatman, because he wanted me to pay him more than I had agreed to pay, and on this occasion I again had the same difficulty, twice as much being demanded at the ship as was agreed upon at the dock; but I was firm and won my point both times. While in Galilee I had crossed the province from sea to sea; I had visited the city in which Jesus spent the greater part of his earth life, and the sea closely connected with several important things in his career. I had ascended Carmel, and from the top of Tabor I had taken an extensive view of the land, and now I was satisfied to drop down the coast and enter Judaea.

CHAPTER V.

SIGHT-SEEING IN JERUSALEM.

Before leaving the ship at Jaffa I was talking with Mr. Ahmed, a gentleman from India, who had spent some time in Egypt, and had traveled extensively. He claimed to be a British subject, and was able to speak several languages. While we were arranging to go ashore together, one of the many boatmen who had come out to the ship picked up my suit-case while my back was turned, and the next thing I saw of it he was taking it down the stairs to one of the small boats. By some loud and emphatic talk I succeeded in getting him to put it out of one boat into another, but he would not bring it back. Mr. Ahmed and I went ashore with another man, whom we paid for carrying us and our baggage. I found the suit-case on the dock, and we were soon in the custom house, where my baggage and passport were both examined, but Mr. Ahmed escaped having his baggage opened by paying the boatman an additional fee. As we arrived in Jaffa too late to take the train for Jerusalem that day, we waited over night in the city from whence Jonah went to sea so long ago. We lodged at the same hotel and were quartered in the same room. This was the first and only traveling companion I had on the whole journey, and I was a little shy. I felt like I wanted some pledge of honorable dealing from my newly formed acquaintance, and when he expressed himself as being a British subject, I mentioned that I was an American and extended my hand, saying: "Let us treat each other right." He gave me his hand with the words: "Species man, species man!" He meant that we both belonged to the same class of beings, and should, therefore, treat each other right, a very good reason indeed. A long time before, in this same land, Abraham had expressed himself to Lot on a similar line in these words: "Let there be no strife, I pray thee, between me and thee, and between my herdsmen and thy herdsmen; for we are brethren" (Gen. 13:8). On Saturday we moved our baggage over to the depot and boarded the train for Jerusalem. On the way to the depot an old gentleman, whom I would have guessed to be a German, passed me. When I entered the car it was my lot to ride by him. He learned that I had been to Bristol, England, and had visited the orphan homes founded by George Muller, and he remarked: "You are a Christian, then." He probably said this because he thought no other would be interested in such work. It developed that he was a converted Jew, and was conducting a mission for his people in the Holy City. Without telling him my position religiously, I inquired concerning different points, and found his faith and mine almost alike. This new acquaintance was D.C. Joseph, whose association I also enjoyed after reaching Jerusalem.

It was late in the afternoon of October ninth when we got off the train at the Jerusalem station, which is so situated that the city can not be seen from that point. By the time we had our baggage put away in a native hotel outside the city walls it was dark. We then started out to see if there was any mail awaiting me. First we went to the Turkish office, which was reached by a flight of dark stairs. Mr. Ahmed went up rather slowly. Perhaps he felt the need of caution more than I did. According to my recollection, they handed us a candle, and allowed us to inspect the contents of a small case for the mail. We found nothing, so we made our way down the dark stairway to the German office, situated on the ground floor, nicely furnished and properly lighted, but there was no mail there for me, as mail from America goes to the Austrian office, inside the Jaffa gate.

The next day was Lord's day, and for the time being I ceased to be a tourist and gave myself up mainly to religious services. I first attended the meeting conducted by Bro. Joseph at the mission to Israel. It was the first service I had attended, and the first opportunity that had come to me for breaking bread since I left London, the last of August. After this assembly of four persons was dismissed, I went to the services of the Church of England and observed their order of worship. The minister was in a robe, and delivered a really good sermon of about fifteen minutes' duration, preceded by reading prayers and singing praise for about an hour. By invitation, I took dinner with Miss Dunn, an American lady, at whose house Bro. Joseph was lodging. As she had been in Jerusalem fifteen years and was interested in missionary work, I enjoyed her company as well as her cooking. After dinner I went to a little iron-covered meeting-house called the "tabernacle," where a Mr. Thompson, missionary of the Christian Alliance, of Nyack, New York, was the minister. At the close of the Sunday-school a gentleman asked some questions in English, and the native evangelist, Melki, translated them into Arabic. By request of Mr. Thompson, I read the opening lesson and offered prayer, after which he delivered a good address on the great, coming day, and at the close the Lord's Supper was observed. I understood that they did this once a month, but it is attended to weekly at the mission where I was in the morning. At the tabernacle I made the acquaintance of Mr. Stanton, a Methodist minister from the States; Mr. Jennings, a colored minister from Missouri, and Mr. Smith, an American gentleman residing in Jerusalem. There was another meeting in the tabernacle at night, but I staid at the hotel and finished some writing to be sent off to the home land.

Monday was a big day for me. Mr. Ahmed and I went down inside the Jaffa gate and waited for Mr. Smith, who was our guide, Mr. Jennings, and a Mr. Michelson, from California. Mr. Smith had been a farmer in America, but had spent three years at Jerusalem and Jericho. He was well acquainted with the country, and we could depend upon what he told us. Add to all this the fact that he went around with us without charge, and it will be seen that we were well favored. On this Monday morning we started out to take a walk to

Bethany, the old home of that blessed family composed of Mary, Martha, and Lazarus. We passed the Church of the Holy Sepulcher, walked along the street called the Via Dolorosa, and saw several of the "stations" Jesus is supposed to have passed on the way to the execution on Calvary. We passed the traditional site of the "house of the rich man," the "house of the poor man," and the Temple Area. After passing the Church of St. Anne, we went out of the city through St. Stephen's gate, and saw the Birket Sitti Mariam, or Pool of Lady Mary, one hundred feet long, eighty-five feet wide, and once twenty-seven and a half feet deep. It is supposed that Stephen was led through the gate now bearing his name and stoned at a point not far distant. Going down the hill a few rods, we came to the Church of St. Mary, a building for the most part underground. It is entered by a stairway nineteen feet wide at the top, and having forty-seven steps leading to the floor thirty-five feet below. We went down, and in the poorly lighted place we found some priests and others singing or chanting, crossing themselves, kissing a rock, and so on. This church probably gets its name from the tradition that the mother of Jesus was buried here. Just outside the church is a cavern that is claimed by some to be the place of Christ's agony, and by others, who may have given the matter more thought, it is supposed to be an old cistern, or place for storing olive oil or grain. Perhaps I would do well to mention here that tradition has been in operation a long time, and the stories she has woven are numerous indeed, but often no confidence can be placed in them. I desire to speak of things of this kind in such a way as not to mislead my readers. It was near this church that I saw lepers for the first time. The valley of the Kidron is the low ground lying between Jerusalem and the Mount of Olives. The water flows here only in the wet part of the year. Crossing this valley and starting up the slope of the Mount of Olives, we soon come to a plot of ground inclosed by a high stone wall, with a low, narrow gateway on the upper side. This place is of great interest, as it bears the name "Garden of Gethsemane," and is probably the spot to which the lowly Jesus repaired and prayed earnestly the night before his execution, when his soul was "exceeding sorrowful, even unto death." It is really a garden, filled with flowers, and olive trees whose trunks, gnarled and split, represent them as being very old, but it is not to be supposed that they are the same trees beneath which Jesus prayed just before Judas and "the band of soldiers and officers" came out to arrest him. There is a fence inside the wall, leaving a passageway around the garden between the wall and the fence. Where the trees reach over the fence a woven-wire netting has been fixed up, to keep the olives from dropping on the walk, where tourists could pick them up for souvenirs. The fruit of these old trees is turned into olive oil and sold, and the seeds are used in making rosaries. At intervals on the wall there are pictures representing the fourteen stations Jesus passed as he was being taken to the place of crucifixion. This garden is the property of the Roman Catholics, and the Greeks have selected another spot, which they regard as the true Gethsemane, just as each church holds a different place at Nazareth to be the spot where the angry Nazarenes intended to destroy the Savior.

Leaving the garden, we started on up the slope of Olivet, and passed the fine Russian church, with its seven tapering domes, that shine like the gold by which they are said to be covered. It appears to be one of the finest buildings of Jerusalem. As we went on, we looked back and had a good view of the Kidron valley and the Jews' burial place, along the slope of the mountain, where uncounted thousands of Abraham's descendants lie interred. Further up toward the summit is the Church of the Lord's Prayer, a building erected by a French princess, whose body is now buried within its walls. This place is peculiar on account of at least two things. That portion of Scripture commonly called "the Lord's prayer" is here inscribed on large marble slabs in thirty-two different languages, and prayer is said to be offered here continually. There is another church near the Damascus gate, where two "sisters" are said to be kneeling in prayer at all hours. I entered the beautiful place at different times, and always found it as represented, but it should not be supposed that the same women do all the praying, as they doubtless have enough to change at regular intervals. The Church of the Creed is, according to a worthless tradition, the place where the apostles drew up "the creed." It is under the ground, and we passed over it on the way to the Church of the Lord's Prayer. The Mount of Olives is two thousand seven hundred and twenty-three feet above sea level, and is about two hundred feet higher than Mount Moriah. From the summit a fine view of Jerusalem and the surrounding country may be obtained. The Russians have erected a lofty stone tower here. After climbing the spiral stairway leading to the top of it, one is well rewarded by the extensive view. Looking out from the east side, we could gaze upon the Dead Sea, some twenty miles away, and more than four thousand feet below us. We visited the chambers called the "Tombs of the Prophets," but the name is not a sufficient guarantee to warrant us in believing them to be the burial places of the men by whom God formerly spoke to the people. On the way to Bethany we passed the reputed site of Beth-page (Mark 11:1), and soon came to the town where Jesus performed the great miracle of raising Lazarus after he had been dead four days. (John 11:1-46.) The place pointed out as the tomb corresponds to the Scripture which says "It was a cave" where they laid him. Twenty-six steps lead down to the chamber where his body is said to have lain when the "blessed Redeemer" cried with a loud voice, "Lazarus, come forth." Whether this is the exact spot or not, it is probably a very ancient cave. One writer claims that it is as old as the incident itself, and says these rock-cut tombs are the oldest landmarks of Palestine. Tradition points out the home of Lazarus, and there is a portion of an old structure called the Castle of Lazarus, which Lazarus may never have seen. Bethany is a small village, occupied by a few

Mohammedan families, who dislike the "Christians." On the rising ground above the village stands a good modern stone house, owned by an English lady, who formerly lived in it, but her servant, a Mohammedan, made an effort to cut her throat, and almost succeeded in the attempt. Naturally enough, the owner does not wish to live there now, so we found the building in the care of a professing Christian, who treated us with courtesy, giving us a good, refreshing drink, and permitting us to go out on the roof to look around.

From this point we turned our footsteps toward Jerusalem, "about fifteen furlongs off"—that is, about two miles distant. (John 11:18.) When we reached the lower part of the slope of Olivet, where the tombs of departed Jews are so numerous, Mr. Michelson and Mr. Jennings went on across the Kidron valley and back to their lodging places, while Mr. Ahmed, Mr. Smith and I went down to Job's well, in the low ground below the city. The Tower of Absalom, the Tomb of James, and the Pyramid of Zachariah were among the first things we saw. They are all burial places, but we can not depend upon them being the actual tombs of those whose names they bear. The first is a peculiar monument nineteen and one-half feet square and twenty-one feet high, cut out of the solid rock, and containing a chamber, which may be entered by crawling through a hole in the side. On the top of the natural rock portion a structure of dressed stone, terminating in one tapering piece, has been erected, making the whole height of the monument forty-eight feet. The Jews have a custom of pelting it with stones on account of Absalom's misconduct, and the front side shows the effect of their stone-throwing. The Grotto of St. James is the traditional place of his concealment from the time Jesus was arrested till his resurrection. The Pyramid of Zachariah is a cube about thirty feet square and sixteen feet high, cut out of the solid rock, and surmounted by a small pyramid. It has many names cut upon it in Hebrew letters, and there are some graves near by, as this is a favorite burial place. Some of the bodies have been buried between the monument and the wall around it in the passage made in cutting it out of the rock. Going on down the valley, we have the village of Siloam on the hill at our left, and on the other side of the Kidron, the southeastern part of the Holy City. St. Mary's Well is soon reached. This spring, which may be the Gihon of 1 Kings 1:33, is much lower than the surface of the ground, the water being reached by two flights of stairs, one containing sixteen steps, the other fourteen. The spring is intermittent, and flows from three to five times daily in winter. It flows twice a day in summer, but in the autumn it only flows once in the day. When I was there, the spring was low, and two Turkish soldiers were on duty to preserve order among those who came to get water.

The Pool of Siloam, fifty-two feet long and eighteen feet wide, is farther down the valley. The spring and the pool are about a thousand feet apart, and are connected by an aqueduct through the hill, which, owing to imperfect engineering, is seventeen hundred feet long. From a Hebrew inscription found in the lower end of this passageway it was learned that the excavation was carried on from both ends. A little below the Pool of Siloam the valley of the Kidron joins the valley of Hinnom, where, in ancient times, children were made "to pass through the fire to Moloch" (2 Kings 23:10). Job's Well, perhaps the En Rogel, on the northern border of Judah (Joshua 15:7), is rectangular in shape and one hundred and twenty-three feet deep. Sometimes it overflows, but it seldom goes dry. When I saw it, no less than six persons were drawing water with ropes and leather buckets. The location of Aceldama, the field of blood, has been disputed, but some consider that it was on the hill above the valley of Hinnom. There are several rock-cut tombs along the slope of the hill facing the valley of Hinnom, and some of them are being used as dwelling places. The Moslems have charge of a building outside the city walls, called David's Tomb, which they guard very carefully, and only a portion of it is accessible to visitors. Near this place a new German Catholic church was being erected at a cost of four hundred thousand dollars. We entered the city by the Zion gate, and passed the Tower of David, a fortification on Mount Zion, near the Jaffa gate.

On the ship coming down from Beyrout I had a conversation with a man who claimed to have been naturalized in the United States, and to have gone to Syria to visit his mother, but, according to his story, he was arrested and imprisoned by the Turks. After being mistreated in the filthy prison for some time, he secured his release by bribing a soldier to post a letter to one of the American authorities. He expressed a desire to visit Jerusalem, but seemed afraid to get back into Turkish territory. Learning that I was going there, he wrote a letter to the Armenian Patriarch, and I presented it one day. In a few minutes Mr. Ahmed and I were led into the large room where the Patriarch was seated in his robe and peculiar cap. Meeting a dignitary of the Armenian Church was a new experience to me. I shook hands with him; Mr. Ahmed made some signs and sat down. In the course of our limited conversation he said rather slowly: "I am very old." Replying to a question, he informed me that his age was eighty years. I was on the point of leaving, but he hindered me, and an attendant soon came in with some small glasses of wine and a little dish of candy. The Patriarch drank a glass of wine, and I took a piece of the candy, as also did Mr. Ahmed, and then we took our leave.

The eleventh day of October, which was Tuesday, was occupied with a trip to Hebron, described in another chapter devoted to the side trips I made from Jerusalem, but the next day was spent in looking around the Holy City. Early in the morning the Mamilla Pool, probably the "upper pool" of 2 Kings 18:17, was seen. One author gives the dimensions of this pool as follows: Length, two hundred and ninety-one feet; breadth, one hundred and ninety-two feet; depth, nineteen feet. It is filled with water in the rainy season, but was empty when I saw it. Entering the city by the Jaffa gate, I walked along David and Christian Streets, and was shown the Pool of Hezekiah, which is surrounded by houses, and was supplied from the Mamilla Pool.

The next place visited was that interesting old building, the Church of the Holy Sepulcher, where our Lord is supposed to have been buried in Joseph's new tomb. Jerusalem has many things of great interest, but some few things are of special interest. The Temple Area and Calvary are of this class. I am sure my readers will want to know something of each, and I shall here write of the latter. No doubt the spot where Jesus was crucified and the grave in which he was buried were both well known to the brethren up to the destruction of the city in the year seventy. Before this awful calamity the Christians made their escape, and when they returned they "would hardly recognize the fallen city as the one they had left; the heel of the destroyer had stamped out all semblance of its former glory. For sixty years it lay in ruins so complete that it is doubtful if there was a single house that could be used as a residence; during these years its history is a blank." There is no mention of the returned Christians seeking out the site of either the crucifixion or burial, and between A.D. 120 and A.D. 136 Hadrian reconstructed the city, changing it to a considerable extent, and naming it Aelia Capitolina. This would tend to make the location of Calvary more difficult. Hadrian built a temple to Venus, probably on the spot now occupied by the Church of the Holy Sepulchre, and Eusebius, writing about A.D. 325, speaks of Constantine's church built on the site of this temple. It is claimed that Hadrian's heathen temple was erected to desecrate the place of Christ's entombment, and that Constantine's church, being erected on the site of the temple, and regarded as the place called Calvary, fixes this as the true site; but whether the church and temple were on the same site or not, the present church stands where the one built by Constantine stood, and is regarded by the mass of believers as the true location.

Constantine's church stood two hundred and eighty years, being destroyed by Chosroes II., of Persia, in A.D. 614, but was soon succeeded by another structure not so grand as its predecessor. In 1010, in the "reign of the mad caliph Hakem," the group of churches was entirely destroyed, and the spot lay desolate for thirty years, after which another church was erected, being completed in eight years. This building was standing in 1099, the time of the Crusaders, but was destroyed by fire in 1808. This fire "consumed many of the most sacred relics in the church. Marble columns of great age and beauty crumbled in the flames. The rich hangings and pictures were burned, along with lamps and chandeliers and other ornaments in silver and gold. The lead with which the great dome was lined melted, and poured down in streams." The building now standing there was finished in 1810 at a cost of nearly three millions of dollars, one-third of this, it is said, being expended in lawsuits and Mohammedan bribes. It is the property of several denominations, who adorn their separate chapels to suit themselves.

The church is entered from a court having two doors or gates. Worshipers pass through the court, and stop at the left-hand side of the door and kiss the marble column, which clearly shows the effect of this practice. Just inside of the building there is a guard, composed of members of the oldest Mohammedan family in the city. The reader may wonder why an armed guard should be kept in a church house, but such a reader has not seen or read of all the wickedness that is carried on in the support of sectarianism. Concerning this guard, which, at the time of the holy fire demonstration, is increased by several hundred soldiers, Edmund Sherman Wallace, a former United States Consul in this city, says in his "Jerusalem the Holy": "This Christian church has a Moslem guard, whose duty it is to keep peace among the various sects who profess belief in the Prince of Peace. * * * It is a sickening fact that Moslem brute force must compel Christians to exercise, not charity toward each other, but common decency and decorum. But it is a fact nevertheless, and will remain apparent to all so long as priestcraft takes the place of New Testament Christianity and superstition supplants religion."

A little beyond this guard is the "Stone of Unction," upon which many believe Jesus was prepared for burial, but the original stone for which this claim was made is not now visible, being covered with the present slab to keep it from being worn out by the kissing of pious pilgrims. It is eight and a half feet long and four feet wide. Pilgrims sometimes bring the goods for their burial robes here and measure them by this stone. Some large candles stand by it, and above it are eight fine lamps, belonging to the Greek and Roman Catholics, the Copts, and Armenians. Not far away is a small stone, which I understood was called the place where the women watched the preparation by Joseph of Arimathea and Nicodemus. (John 19:38-42.)

In the center of the rotunda, with its entrance facing the east, is the Chapel of the Sepulcher, the holiest place in all this holy building. Passing through the small door, the visitor finds himself in the Chapel of the Angels, a very small room, where a piece of stone, said to have been rolled away from the grave by the angels, is to be seen. Stooping down, the visitor passes through a low opening and enters the Chapel of the Sepulcher proper, a room only six and a half feet long and six feet wide. The "tomb" is at the right hand of the entrance, occupying about half of the floor, above which it rises two feet. It is covered with marble, so that even if this were the very spot where the Lord and Savior was laid by the hands of kind friends, the modern visitor would not know what it looked like when that event took place. The little chapel, capable of accommodating about six people at a time, contains some pictures and forty-three silver lamps, the property of the Copts, Armenians,

Greek and Roman Catholics. A priest stands on guard, so that no damage may be done to any part of the place.

The Greek chapel, the largest, and to my notion the finest that I saw, is just in front of the sepulcher. From its having two sections and a partition, I was reminded of the tabernacle of the wilderness journey. Services were being conducted once while I was there, and I saw the Patriarch and others, gorgeously robed, going through with a service that was at least spectacular, if not spiritual. At one point in the exercises those participating came down close to where I was standing, passed around the spot designated "the center of the world," and went back again to the farther end of the richly ornamented room. One of the priests, with hair reaching down on his shoulders, bore a silver vessel, which I suppose contained burning incense. The long hair, beautiful robes, the singing, praying, and such things, made up a service that reminded me of the days of Solomon and the old priesthood.

The demonstration of the "holy fire" takes place in this church once a year, and there are thousands who believe that the fire passed out from the Chapel of the Angels really comes from heaven. This occurs on the Saturday afternoon preceding Easter, and the eager, waiting throng, a part of which has been in the building since the day before, soon has its hundreds of little candles lighted. As the time for the appearance of the fire approaches the confusion becomes greater. Near the entrance to the sepulcher a group of men is repeating the words: "This is the tomb of Jesus Christ;" not far from them others are saying: "This is the day the Jew mourns and the Christian rejoices;" others express themselves in the language: "Jesus Christ has redeemed us;" and occasionally "God save the Sultan" can be heard.

Mr. Wallace, from whose book the foregoing items are gleaned, in telling of a fight which took place at one stage of the service, describes it as "a mass of wriggling, struggling, shrieking priests and soldiers, each apparently endeavoring to do all the possible injury to whomever he could reach. * * * But the fight went on. Greek trampled on Armenian, and Armenian on Greek, and Turk on both. Though doing his very best, the commanding officer seemed unable to separate the combatants. The bugle rang out time after time, and detachment after detachment of soldiers plunged into the mêlee. * * * This went on for fifteen minutes. Just how much damage was done nobody will ever know. There were a number of bruised faces and broken heads, and a report was current that two pilgrims had died from injuries received." This disgraceful and wicked disturbance is said to have been brought about by the Armenians wanting two of their priests to go with the Greek Patriarch as far as the Chapel of the Angels. And it is furthermore said that the defeat of the Armenians was brought about, to some extent at least, by the muscular strength of an American professional boxer and wrestler, whom the Greeks had taken along in priestly garb as a member of the Patriarch's bodyguard. It is not surprising that Mr. Wallace has written: "The Church of the Holy Sepulcher gives the non-Christian world the worst possible illustration of the religion of Him in whose name it stands."

As I was going through the city, I saw a camel working an olive press. The poor blindfolded animal was compelled to walk in a circle so small that the outside trace was drawn tightly over its leg, causing irritation; but seeing the loads that are put upon dumb brutes, and men too, sometimes, one need not expect much attention to be given to the comfort of these useful servants. Truly, there is great need for the refining, civilizing, and uplifting influence of the gospel here in the city where it had its earliest proclamation. I also visited two grist mills operated by horses on a treadmill, which was a large wooden wheel turned on its side, so the horses could stand on it. I was not pleased with the nearness of the manure in one of these mills to the material from which the "staff of life" is made.

The German Protestant Church of the Redeemer is a fine structure on the Muristan, completed in 1898. The United States consulate is near the Austrian postoffice inside of the Jaffa gate. I went there and rested awhile, but saw the consul, Selah Merrill, at his hotel, where I also met Mrs. Merrill, and formed a favorable opinion of both of them. Here I left my belt, checks, and surplus money in the care of the consul.

Continuing my walk on Wednesday, I passed one of the numerous threshing floors of the country. This one was the face of a smooth rock, but they are often the ground on some elevated spot, where a good breeze can be had to blow away the chaff, for the grain is now threshed and cleaned by the primitive methods of long ago. After the grain has been tramped out (1 Cor. 9:9), the straw, now worn to chaff, is piled up, and when a favorable wind blows, a man tosses it in the air with a wooden fork. The grain falls in a pile at his feet and the chaff is carried aside some distance. When this operation has been carried on as long as is profitable, the wheat and what chaff remains in it are thrown into the air with a wooden shovel, called in our Bibles a "fan." (Matt. 3:12.) The final cleaning is done by washing the grain, or with a sieve.

The Tombs of the Kings, which may never have contained a king, are extensive and interesting. They are surrounded by a wall, and to reach them the visitor must go down a very wide stairway. The steps probably do not number more than twenty-five, but the distance from one side of the stairs to the other is twenty-seven feet. There are channels cut in the rock to carry the water that comes down these steps to the cisterns, two in number, one of which is a good-sized room cut in the rock at the side of the stairway. It contained about three feet of water when I saw it, although there had been no rain in Jerusalem for half a year. The other one, at the bottom of the stairs, is much larger, and was empty. The vaulted roof is supported by a column, and there are steps leading from one level of the floor to another.

Turning to the left at the foot of the big stairway, we passed through an arch cut through the rock into a court made by excavating the earth and stone to a depth of perhaps twenty feet. It is ninety feet long and eighty-one feet wide. The entrance to the tombs is by a vestibule cut in the rock at one side of the court, and it appears that this once had a row of pillars along the front, like veranda posts. We went down a few steps and stooped low enough to pass through an opening about a yard high. Beyond this we found ourselves in a good-sized room, cut in the solid rock. There are five of these rooms, and so far as the appearance is concerned, one might suppose they had been made in modern times, but they are ancient. The bodies were usually buried in "pigeon-holes" cut back in the walls of the rooms, but there are some shelf tombs, which are sufficiently described in their name. One room seems never to have been completed, but there are burial places here for about forty people.

One of the interesting things about these tombs is the rolling stone by which they were closed. It is a round rock, resembling a millstone. The height is a little over three feet and a half, and the thickness sixteen inches. It stands in a channel cut for the purpose, but was rolled forward before the entrance when it was desirable to have the tombs closed. When Jesus was buried, a "great stone" was rolled to the mouth of the sepulcher, and the women thought of this as they went to the tomb on the first day of the week, saying: "Who shall roll us away the stone from the door of the tomb?" (Mark 16:3.) They went on and found the tomb open; so, also, we may often find the stone rolled away if we will go forward in the discharge of our duties, instead of sitting down to mourn at the thought of something in the distance which seems too difficult.

On our way to the tombs just mentioned, we passed the American Colony, a small band of people living together in a rather peculiar manner, but they are not all Americans. I understood that there had been no marriages among them for a long time until a short while before I was in Jerusalem. Some of them conduct a good store near the Jaffa gate. We passed an English church and college and St. Stephen's Church on the way to Gordon's Calvary. This new location of the world's greatest tragedy is a small hill outside the walls on the northern side of the city. The Church of the Holy Sepulcher stands on ground which for fifteen hundred years has been regarded as the true site of our Lord's death and burial, but since Korte, a German bookseller, visited the city in 1738, doubts have been expressed as to the correctness of the tradition. Jesus "suffered without the gate" (Heb. 13:12), and "in the place where he was crucified there was a garden; and in the garden a new tomb wherein was man never yet laid" (John 19:41), and it appears to have been near a public road. (Mark 15:29.) In 1856 Edward Robinson, an American, offered proof that the site sustained by the old tradition was inside the city walls at the time of the crucifixion, and more recent discoveries, made in excavating, confirm his proof. The new Calvary meets the requirements of the above mentioned scriptures, and gets its name "Gordon's Calvary," from the fact that General Gordon wrote and spoke in favor of this being the correct location, and a photographer attached his name to a view of the place. In the garden adjoining the new Calvary I visited a tomb, which some suppose to be the place of our Lord's burial.

On the way back to my lodging place we passed the Damascus gate, the most attractive of all the old city gates, and one often represented in books. It was built or repaired in 1537, and stands near an older gateway that is almost entirely hidden by the accumulated rubbish of centuries, only the crown of the arch now showing. As we went on we passed the French Hospice, a fine modern building, having two large statues on it. The higher one represents the Virgin and her child, the other is a figure of the Savior. The Catholic church already mentioned, where two sisters are to be seen in prayer at all times, is near the Hospice. It is a rather impressive sight to stand in this beautiful but silent place, and see those women in white robes kneeling there almost as motionless as statues.

Thursday and a part of Friday was taken up with a trip to Jericho, but we got back in time to spend the afternoon in looking around Jerusalem, and we had an interesting visit to the home of Mrs. Schoenecke, a German lady, whose father, named Schick, spent fifty-six years of his life in Jerusalem. From what information Mr. Schick could gather from the Bible, Josephus, the Talmud, and his personal observations during the time the Palestine Exploration Fund was at work, he constructed large models of the ancient temples that stood on Mount Moriah from the days of Solomon to the time of Herod and Christ. I was told that the original models were sold to an American college for five thousand dollars. Mr. Schick then constructed the models shown to us, and explained by Mrs. Schoenecke. We were also shown a model of the tabernacle used while Israel was marching to the promised land.

The Wailing Place is a rectangle one hundred feet long by fifteen feet wide on the outside of the Temple Area, on the western side, where the wall is about sixty feet high. Some of the stones in this section are of large size, and authorities admit that they are of Solomon's time, but the wall in which they now stand may be a reconstruction. The Jews come here on the Sabbath, beginning at sundown on Saturday, for a service which one author describes as follows: "Nearest to him stood a row of women clad in robes of spotless white. Their eyes were bedimmed with weeping, and tears streamed down their cheeks as they sobbed aloud with irrepressible emotion. Next to the women stood a group of Pharisees—Jews from Poland and Germany. * * *

The old hoary-headed men generally wore velvet caps edged with fur, long love-locks or ringlets dangling on their thin cheeks, and their outer robes presented a striking contrast of gaudy colors. Beyond stood a group of Spanish Jews. * * * Besides these there are Jews from every quarter of the world, who had wandered back to Jerusalem that they might die in the city of their fathers, and be buried in the Valley of Jehoshaphat, under the shadow of the Temple Hill. The worshipers gradually increased in number until the crowd thronging the pavement could not be fewer than two hundred. It was an affecting scene to notice their earnestness; some thrust their hands between the joints of the stones, and pushed into the crevices, as far as possible, little slips of paper, on which were written, in the Hebrew tongue, short petitions addressed to Jehovah. Some even prayed with their mouths thrust into the gaps, where the weather-beaten stones were worn away at the joints. * * * The congregation at the Wailing Place is one of the most solemn gatherings left to the Jewish Church, and, as the writer gazed at the motley concourse, he experienced a feeling of sorrow that the remnants of the chosen race should be heartlessly thrust outside the sacred inclosure of their fathers' holy temple by men of an alien race and an alien creed." So far as I know, all writers give these worshipers credit for being sincere, but on the two occasions when I visited the place, I saw no such emotion as described in the foregoing quotation. The following lines are often rehearsed, the leader reading one at a time, after which the people respond with the words: "We sit in solitude and mourn."

"For the place that lies desolate;
For the place that is destroyed;
For the walls that are overthrown;
For our majesty that is departed;
For our great men who lie dead;
For the precious stones that are buried;
For the priests who have stumbled;
For our kings who have despised Him."

This solemn practice has been observed for about twelve hundred years, but the same place may not have been used all the time. "She is become a widow, that was great among the nations! She that was a princess among the provinces is become tributary! Jerusalem hath grievously sinned; therefore she is become as an unclean thing" (Lam. 1: 1, 8).

On Friday evening we entered some of the many synagogues yet to be found in Jerusalem and observed the worshipers. On Saturday we went to the House of Industry of the English church, where boys are taught to work. Olive wood products are made for the tourist trade. We passed a place where some men were making a peculiar noise as they were pounding wheat and singing at their work. This pounding was a part of the process of making it ready for food. An old lady was standing in an open door spinning yarn in a very simple manner. We watched her a few minutes, and I wanted to buy the little arrangement with which she was spinning, but she didn't care to part with it. She brought out another one, and let me have it after spinning a few yards upon it. I gave her a Turkish coin worth a few cents, for which she seemed very thankful, and said, as Mr. Ahmed explained: "God bless you and give you long life. I am old, and may die to-day." She told us that she came from Mosul, away beyond the Syrian desert, to die in Jerusalem. We visited the synagogue of the Caraite Jews, a small polygamous sect, numbering in this assembly about thirty persons. They also differ from the majority of Hebrews in rejecting the Talmud, but I believe they have a Talmud of their own. Their place of worship is a small room almost under the ground, where we were permitted to see a very fine old copy of the Hebrew Scriptures, our Old Testament. The work was done by hand, and I was told the man who did it was sixteen years of age when he began it, and was sixty when he finished the work, and that the British Museum had offered five thousand dollars for the book. Some of these people speak English, and we conversed with one woman who was quite intelligent. They kindly permitted us to go up and view the city from the housetop.

In the afternoon we visited the Temple Area, an inclosure of about thirty-five acres, in the southeastern part of the city, including the Mosque of Omar (more appropriately called the Dome of the Rock), the Mosque El Aksa, and Solomon's Stables. For Christians to enter this inclosure, it is necessary to notify their consul and secure the service of his *cavasse*, an armed guard, and a Turkish soldier, both of whom must be paid for their services. Thus equipped, we entered the inclosure, and came up on the east front of the Dome of the Rock, probably so named from the fact that the dome of this structure stands over an exposed portion of the natural rock, fifty-seven feet long, forty-three feet wide, and rising a few feet above the floor. After putting some big slippers on over our shoes, we entered the building and saw this great rock, which tradition says is the threshing floor of Araunah, and the spot where Melchizedek sacrificed. It is also the traditional place where Abraham sacrificed Isaac, and it is believed that David built an altar here after the angel of destruction had put up his sword. It is furthermore supposed that the great altar of burnt offerings stood on this rock in the days of Solomon's Temple, which is thought to have been located just west of it. This is the probable location of Zerubbabel's Temple, and the one enlarged and beautified by Herod, which was standing when Jesus was on earth, and continued to stand until the awful destruction of the city by the Roman army in A.D. 70.

The modern visitor to this fine structure would have no thought of the ancient temple of God if he depended upon what he sees here to suggest it.

All trace of that house has disappeared. The Dome of the Rock, said to be "the most beautiful piece of architecture in Jerusalem," belongs to the Turks. It has eight sides, each about sixty-six and a half feet long, and is partly covered with marble, but it is, to some extent, in a state of decay. Between the destruction of the temple and the erection of this building a heathen temple and a church had been built on the spot.

The Mosque El Aksa was also visited, but it is noted more for its size than the beauty of its architecture. The Turkish Governor of Palestine comes here every Friday to worship at the time the Sultan is engaged in like manner in Constantinople. Solomon's Stables next engaged our attention. We crossed the Temple Area to the wall on the southeastern border, and went down a stairway to these underground chambers, which were made by building about a hundred columns and arching them over and laying a pavement on the top, thereby bringing it up on a level with the rest of the hill. The vaults are two hundred and seventy-three feet long, one hundred and ninety-eight feet wide, and about thirty feet high. They were not made for stables, but were used for that purpose in the middle ages, and the holes through the corners of the square stone columns show where the horses were tied. A large portion of these chambers has been made into a cistern or reservoir.

After a visit to what is called the Pool of Bethesda and the Church of St. Anne, we went outside the city wall on the north side and entered what looks like a cave, but upon investigation proves to be an extensive underground quarry. These excavations, called Solomon's Quarries, extend, according to one authority, seven hundred feet under the hill Bezetha, which is north of Mt. Moriah. The rock is very white, and will take some polish. Loose portions of it are lying around on the floor of the cavern, and there are distinct marks along the sides where the ancient stone-cutters were at work. In one part of the quarries we were shown the place where visiting Masons are said to hold lodge meetings sometimes. Vast quantities of the rock have been taken out, and this is probably the source from whence much of the building material of the old city was derived.

The trip to the quarries ended my sight-seeing for the week. The next morning I went to the Church of the Holy Sepulcher and witnessed a part of the service of the Greek Catholics. At a later hour I went around to the mission conducted by Bro. Joseph, and, with the little congregation there assembled, broke bread in memory of Him who in this city, almost two thousand years ago, gave his life for the sins of the world, after having instituted this supper, a monumental institution, representing to our minds the cost of the world's redemption. In the afternoon I attended the preaching service in Mr. Thompson's tabernacle, and visited the Abyssinian church, near Mr. Smith's house. This Abyssinian house is circular, and has a small, round room in the center, around which the congregation stands and worships, leaning on their staves, for the place is void of seats. At night I preached in the tabernacle on the question: "What must I do to be saved?" Melki, the native evangelist, translated for me as I went along, and the congregation paid good attention and seemed pleased to have heard me. I know I am pleased to have had opportunity to "preach the word" in the city from whence it was first published to the world.

One of the first sights beheld when I started out on Monday morning was a foundation, laid at the expense of a woman who intended to build a house for the "hundred and forty-four thousand." It represents one of the many peculiar religious ideas that find expression in and around Jerusalem. We went on to the railway station, where I saw a young man, a Jew, leave for that far-off land called America. Next the Leper Hospital was visited. This well-kept institution is in the German colony, and had several patients of both sexes. A lady, who spoke some English, kindly showed me through the hospital, and explained that the disease is not contagious, but hereditary, and that some lepers refuse to enter the hospital because they are forbidden to marry. The patients were of various ages, and showed the effects of the disease in different stages. In some cases it makes the victim a sad sight to look upon. I remember one of these poor, afflicted creatures, whose face was almost covered with swollen and inflamed spots. Some were blind, and some had lost part or all of their fingers by the disease. One man's nose was partly consumed.

At Bishop Gobat's school we were kindly received, and given a good, refreshing drink. The founder of this school, a member of the English church, was one of the pioneers in Jerusalem mission work, and stood very high in the estimation of the people. His grave is to be seen in the cemetery near the school, where one may also see the supposed site of the ancient city wall. Besides the Leper Hospital, we visited another hospital under German control, where patients may have medical attention and hospital service for the small sum of one *mejidi*, about eighty cents, for a period, of fifteen days, but higher fees are charged in other departments. We soon reached the English hospital, maintained by the Society for the Promotion of Christianity among the Jews. It is built on a semi-circular plan in such a way that the wards, extending back from the front, admit light from both sides. This institution is free to the Jews, but I understand Mohammedans were not admitted without a fee.

The Syrian Orphanage had about three hundred children in it, who were being instructed in books and in manual labor. Those who can see are taught to work in wood, to make a kind of tile used in constructing partitions, and other lines of useful employment. They had some blind children, who were being taught to make baskets and brushes. On the way back to Mr. Smith's I stopped at the Jewish Library, a small two-story building, having the books and papers upstairs. They have a raised map of Palestine, which was interesting to me, after having twice crossed the country from sea to sea.

The last Thursday I was in the city I went with some friends to the Israelite Alliance School, an institution with about a thousand pupils, who receive both an industrial and a literary education. We were conducted through the school by a Syrian gentleman named Solomon Elia, who explained that, while the institution is under French control, English is taught to some extent, as some of the pupils would go to Egypt, where they would need to use this language. The boys are instructed in wood-working, carpentry, copper-working, and other lines of employment. We saw some of the girls making hair nets, and others were engaged in making lace. Both of these products are sent out of Palestine for sale. The institution has received help from some of the Rothschild family, and I have no doubt that it is a great factor for the improvement of those who are reached by it. Jerusalem is well supplied with hospitals and schools. The Greek and Roman Catholic churches, the Church of England, and numerous other religious bodies have a footing here, and are striving to make it stronger. Their schools and hospitals are made use of as missionary agencies, and besides these there is a Turkish hospital and numerous Mohammedan schools.

On Friday I had an opportunity to see a man measuring grain, as is indicated by the Savior's words: "Give, and it shall be given unto you; good measure, pressed down, shaken together, running over, shall they give into your bosom. For with what measure ye mete, it shall be measured to you again" (Luke 6:38). He filled his measure about full, and then shook it down thoroughly. He next filled it up and shook it down until he evidently thought he had all he could get that way, so he commenced to pile it up on top. When he had about as much heaped up as would stay on, he put his hands on the side of the cone opposite himself and gently pulled it toward him. He then piled some more on the far side, and when he had reached the limit in this way, he carefully leveled the top of the cone down a little, and when he could no longer put on more grain, he gently lifted the measure and moved it around to the proper place, where it was quickly dumped. In the evening Mr. Smith and I walked out on Mount Scopus, where Titus had his camp at the time of the siege and destruction of Jerusalem, as foretold by our Lord and Master in the twenty-fourth of Matthew.

As we went along, Mr. Smith pointed out the watershed between the Mediterranean and the Dead Sea. The view from Scopus is very extensive. We could look away to the north to Nebi Samwil, where the Prophet Samuel is supposed by some to have been buried. Ramallah, the seat of a school maintained by the Society of Friends, is pointed out, along with Bireh, Bethel, and Geba. Nob, the home of the priests slain by command of Saul (1 Samuel 22:16), and Anathoth, one of the cities of refuge (Joshua 21:18), are in sight.

Swinging on around the circle to the east, the northern end of the Dead Sea is visible, while the Mount of Olives is only a little distance below us. Across the valley of the Kidron lies the Holy City, with her walls constructed at various periods and under various circumstances, her dome-shaped stone roofs, synagogues, mosques, and minarets, being "trodden down of the Gentiles, until the times of the Gentiles be fulfilled" (Luke 21:24). Here, with this panorama spread out in the evening light, I may say my sight-seeing in the City of the Great King came to an end.

I lacked but a few hours of having been in the city two weeks, when I boarded the train for Jaffa on my way to Egypt. The most of the time I had lodged in the hospitable home of Mr. Smith, where I had a clean and comfortable place to rest my tired body when the shadows of night covered the land. I had received kind treatment, and had seen many things of much interest. I am truly thankful that I have been permitted to make this trip to Jerusalem. Let me so live that when the few fleeting days of this life are over, I may rest with the redeemed. When days and years are no more, let me enjoy, in the NEW JERUSALEM, the blessedness that remains for those that have loved the Lord.

"And I saw the holy city, new Jerusalem, coming down out of heaven from God, made ready as a bride adorned for her husband. And I heard a great voice out of the throne saying, Behold, the tabernacle of God is with men, and he shall dwell with them, and they shall be his peoples, and God himself shall be with them, and be their God: and he shall wipe away every tear from their eyes; and death shall be no more; neither shall there be mourning, nor crying, nor pain, any more: the first things have passed away" (Revelation 21:2-4).

CHAPTER VI.

SIDE TRIPS FROM JERUSALEM.

Early on Tuesday morning, the eleventh of October, I set out by carriage, with some other tourists, for a trip to Bethlehem, Solomon's Pools, and Hebron. Bethlehem is about five miles south of Jerusalem, and Hebron is a little southwest of the Holy City and twenty miles distant. We started from the Jaffa gate and passed the Sultan's Pool, otherwise known as Lower Gihon, which may be the "lower pool" of Isaiah 22:9. "The entire area of this pool," says one writer, "is about three and a half acres, with an average depth, when clear of deposit, of forty-two and a half feet in the middle from end to end." We drove for two miles, or perhaps more, across the Plain of Rephaim, one of David's battlefields soon after he established himself in Jerusalem. Here he was twice victorious over the Philistines. In the first instance he asked Jehovah: "Shall I go up against the Philistines? Wilt thou deliver them into my hand?" The answer was: "Go up; for I will certainly deliver the Philistines into thy hand." In this battle the invaders were routed and driven from the field. "And they left their images there; and David and his men took them away." But "the Philistines came up yet again, and spread themselves in the valley of Rephaim. And when David inquired of Jehovah, he said, Thou shalt not go up: make a circuit behind them, and come upon them over against the mulberry trees. And it shall be, when thou hearest the sound of marching in the tops of the mulberry trees, that then thou shalt bestir thyself, for then is Jehovah gone out before thee to smite the hosts of the Philistines." David obeyed the voice of the Lord, and smote his enemies from Geba to Gezer. (2 Samuel 5:17-25.)

On the southern border of the plain stands the Greek convent called Mar Elyas. This is about half way to Bethlehem, and the city of the nativity soon comes into view. Before going much farther the traveler sees a well-built village, named Bet Jala, lying on his right. It is supposed to be the ancient Giloh, mentioned in 2 Samuel 15:12 as the home of Ahithophel, David's counselor, for whom Absalom sent when he conspired against his father. Here the road forks, one branch of it passing Bet Jala and going on to Hebron; the other, bearing off to the left, leads directly to Bethlehem, which we passed, intending to stop there as we returned in the evening. At this place we saw the monument erected to mark the location of Rachel's tomb, a location, like many others, in dispute. When Jacob "journeyed from Bethel and there was still some distance to come to Ephrath," Rachel died at the birth of Benjamin, "and was buried in the way to Ephrath (the same is Bethlehem). * * * And Jacob set up a pillar upon her grave" (Gen. 35:16-20). The spot, which for many centuries was marked by a pyramid of stones, is now occupied by a small stone building with a dome-shaped roof, at the east side of which is a room, open on the north, with a flat roof. For hundreds of years tradition has located the grave at this place, which is indeed near Bethlehem, but in 1 Samuel 10:2 it is mentioned as being "in the border of Benjamin," which has occasioned the belief that the true location is some miles farther north.

Before long we came to Solomon's Pools. We first stopped at a doorway, which looks like it might lead down to a cellar, but in reality the door is at the head of a flight of stairs leading down to what is known as the "sealed fountain" (Song of Solomon 4:12). The door was fastened, and we were not able to descend to the underground chamber, which is forty-one feet long, eleven and a half feet wide, with an arched stone roof, all of which, except the entrance, is below the surface. A large basin cut in the floor collects the water from two springs. After rising a foot in the basin, the water flows out into a channel more than six hundred feet long leading down to the two upper pools. These great reservoirs, bearing the name of Israel's wisest monarch, are still in a good state of preservation, having been repaired in modern times. The first one is three hundred and eighty feet long, two hundred and twenty-nine feet wide at one end, two hundred and thirty feet wide at the other, and twenty-five feet deep. The second pool is four hundred and twenty-three feet long, one hundred and sixty feet wide at the upper end, two hundred and fifty feet wide at the lower end, and thirty-nine feet deep at that end. The third pool is the largest of all, having a length of five hundred and eighty-two feet. The upper end is one hundred and forty-eight feet wide, the lower end two hundred and seven feet, and the depth at the lower end is fifty feet. The pools are about one hundred and fifty feet apart, and have an aggregate area of six and a quarter acres, with an average depth approaching thirty-eight feet. The upper two received water from the sealed fountain, but the lower one was supplied from an aqueduct leading up from a point more than three miles to the south. The aqueduct from the sealed fountain leads past the pools, and winds around the hills to Bethlehem and on to the Temple Area, in Jerusalem. It is still in use as far as Bethlehem, and could be put in repair and made serviceable for the whole distance. An offer to do this was foolishly rejected by the Moslems in 1870. The only habitation near the pools is an old khan, "intended as a stopping place for caravans and as a station for soldiers to guard the road and the pools." The two upper pools were empty when I saw them, but the third one contained some water and a great number of frogs. As we went on to Hebron we got a drink at "Philip's Well," the place where "the eunuch was baptized," according to a tradition which lacks support by the present appearance of the place.

Towards noon we entered the "valley of Eschol," from whence the spies sent out by Moses carried the great cluster of grapes. (Num. 13:23.) Before entering Hebron we turned aside and went up to Abraham's Oak, a very old tree, but not old enough for Abraham to have enjoyed its shade almost four thousand years ago. The trunk is thirty-two feet in circumference, but the tree is not tall like the American oaks. It is now in a dying condition, and some of the branches are supported by props, while the lower part of the trunk is surrounded by a stone wall, and the space inside is filled with earth. The plot of ground on which the tree stands is surrounded by a high iron fence. A little farther up the hill the Russians have a tower, from which we viewed the country, and then went down in the shade near Abraham's Oak and enjoyed our dinner.

Hebron is a very ancient city, having been built seven and a half years before Zoar in Egypt. (Num. 13:22.) Since 1187 it has been under the control of the Mohammedans, who raise large quantities of grapes, many of which are made into raisins. Articles of glass are made in Hebron, but I saw nothing especially beautiful in this line. The manufacture of goat-skin water-bottles is also carried on. Another line of work which I saw being done is the manufacture of a kind of tile, which looks like a fruit jug without a bottom, and is used in building. Hebron was one of the six cities of refuge (Joshua 20:7), and for seven years and a half it was David's capital of Judah. It is very historic. "Abraham moved his tent, and came and dwelt by the oaks of Mamre, which are in Hebron, and built there an altar unto Jehovah." (Gen. 13:18.) When "Sarah died in Kiriath-arba (the same is Hebron), in the land of Canaan, * * * Abraham came to mourn for Sarah, and to weep for her." At this time the worthy progenitor of the Hebrew race "rose up from before his dead, and spoke unto the children of Heth, saying, I am a stranger and a sojourner with you: give me a possession of a burying-place with you, that I may bury my dead out of my sight." The burial place was purchased for "four hundred shekels of silver, current money of the land. * * * And after this Abraham buried Sarah his wife in the cave in the field of Machpelah before Mamre (the same is Hebron), in the land of Canaan" (Gen. 23:1-20). Years after this, when both Abraham and his son Isaac had passed the way of all the earth and had been laid to rest in this cave, the patriarch Jacob in Egypt gave directions for the entombment of his body in this family burial place. "There they buried Abraham and Sarah his wife; there they buried Isaac and Rebekah his wife; and there I buried Leah" (Gen. 49:31), and here, by his own request, Jacob was buried. (Gen. 50:13.) Joshua, the successor of Moses, "utterly destroyed" Hebron (Joshua 10:37), and afterwards gave it to Caleb, to whom it had been promised by Moses forty-five years before. (Joshua 14:6-15.) Here Abner was slain (2 Samuel 3:27), and the murderers of Ishbosheth were put to death. (2 Samuel 4:12.)

The most interesting thing about the town is the "cave of Machpelah," but it is inaccessible to Christians. Between 1167 and 1187 a church was built on the site, now marked by a carefully guarded Mohammedan mosque. It is inclosed by a wall which may have been built by Solomon. We were allowed to go in at the foot of a stairway as far as the seventh step, but might as well have been in the National Capitol at Washington so far as seeing the burial place was concerned. In 1862 the Prince of Wales, now King of England, was admitted. He was accompanied by Dean Stanley, who has described what he saw, but he was permitted neither to examine the monuments nor to descend to the cave below, the real burial chamber. As the body of Jacob was carefully embalmed by the Egyptian method, it is possible that his remains may yet be seen in their long resting place in this Hebron cave. (Gen. 50:1,2.)

Turning back toward Jerusalem, we came to Bethlehem late in the afternoon, and the "field of the shepherds" (Luke 2:8) and the "fields of Boaz" (Ruth 2:4-23) were pointed out. The place of greatest interest is the group of buildings, composed of two churches, Greek and Latin, and an Armenian convent, all built together on the traditional site of the birth of the Lord Jesus. Tradition is here contradicted by authorities partly on the ground that a cave to which entrance is made by a flight of stairs would probably not be used as a stable. This cave is in the Church of St. Mary, said to have been erected in 330 by Constantine. Descending the stairs, we came into the small cavern, which is continually lighted by fifteen silver lamps, the property of the Greeks, Latins, and Armenians, who each have an interest in the place. Beneath an altar, in a semi-circular recess, a silver star has been set in the floor with the Latin inscription: "*Hic de Virgine Maria Jesus Christus Natus est.*" An armed Turkish soldier was doing duty near this "star of Bethlehem" the evening I was there. The well, from which it is said the "three mighty men" drew water for David, was visited. (2 Samuel 23:15.) But the shades of night had settled down upon the little town where our Savior was born, and we again entered our carriages and drove back to Jerusalem, having had a fine day of interesting sight-seeing. On the Wednesday before I left Jerusalem, in the company of Mrs. Bates, I again visited Bethlehem.

Thursday, October thirteenth, was the day we went down to Jericho, the Dead Sea, and the Jordan. The party was made up of the writer, Mr. Ahmed, Mr. Jennings, Mrs. Bates, four school teachers (three ladies and a gentleman) returning from the Philippines, and the guides, Mr. Smith and Ephraim Aboosh. We went in two carriages driven by natives. "A certain man was going down from Jerusalem to Jericho; and he fell among robbers, who stripped him and beat him, and departed, leaving him half dead" (Luke 10:30). This lonely road is still the scene of occasional robberies, and the Turkish Government permits one of its soldiers to accompany the tourist for a fee, but we did not want to take this escort, as neither of the guides feared any danger. Accordingly we took an early start without notifying the soldiers, and reached Jericho, about twenty miles away, in time to visit Elisha's Fountain before dinner. The road leads out past Bethany, down by the

Apostles' Fountain, on past the Khan of the Good Samaritan, and down the mountain to the plain of the Jordan, this section of which is ten miles long and seven miles wide. Before the road reaches the plain, it runs along a deep gorge bearing the name Wady Kelt, the Brook Cherith, where the prophet Elisha was fed by the ravens night and morning till the brook dried up. (1 Kings 17:1-7.) We also saw the remains of an old aqueduct, and of a reservoir which was originally over five hundred feet long and more than four hundred feet wide. Elisha's Fountain is a beautiful spring some distance from the present Jericho. Doubtless it is the very spring whose waters Elisha healed with salt. (2 Kings 2:19-22.) The ground about the Fountain has been altered some in modern times, and there is now a beautiful pool of good, clear water, a delight both to the eye and to the throat of the dusty traveler who has come down from Jerusalem seeing only the brown earth and white, chalky rock, upon which the unveiled sun has been pouring down his heat for hours. The water from the spring now runs a little grist mill a short distance below it.

After dinner, eaten in front of the hotel in Jericho, we drove over to the Dead Sea, a distance of several miles, and soon we were all enjoying a fine bath in the salt water, the women bathing at one place, the men at another. The water contains so much solid matter, nearly three and a third pounds to the gallon, that it is easy to float on the surface with hands, feet and head above the water. One who can swim but little in fresh water will find the buoyancy of the water here so great as to make swimming easy. When one stands erect in it, the body sinks down about as far as the top of the shoulders. Care needs to be taken to keep the water out of the mouth, nose and eyes, as it is so salty that it is very disagreeable to these tender surfaces. Dead Sea water is two and a half pounds heavier than fresh water, and among other things, it contains nearly two pounds of chloride of magnesium, and almost a pound of chloride of sodium, or common salt, to the gallon. Nothing but some very low forms of animal life, unobserved by the ordinary traveler, can live in this sea. The fish that get into it from the Jordan soon die. Those who bathe here usually drive over to the Jordan and bathe again, to remove the salt and other substances that remain on the body after the first bath. The greatest depth of the Dead Sea is a little over thirteen hundred feet. The wicked cities of Sodom and Gomorrah stood here some place, but authorities disagree as to whether they were at the northern or southern end of the sea. In either case every trace of them has been wiped out by the awful destruction poured on them by the Almighty. (Gen. 18:16 to 19:29)

The Jordan where we saw it, near the mouth, and at the time we saw it, the thirteenth of October, was a quiet and peaceful stream, but the water was somewhat muddy. We entered two little boats and had a short ride on the river whose waters "stood, and rose up in one heap, a great way off," that the children of Israel might cross (Joshua 3:14-17), and beneath whose wave the

Lord and Savior Jesus Christ was baptized by the great prophet of the Judaean wilderness. (Matt. 3:13-17.) We also got out a little while on the east bank of the stream, the only time I was "beyond Jordan" while in Palestine. After supper, eaten in Jericho, we went around to a Bedouin encampment, where a dance was being executed—a dance different from any that I had ever seen before. One of the dancers, with a sword in hand, stood in the center of the ground they were using, while the others stood in two rows, forming a right angle. They went through with various motions and hand-clapping, accompanied by an indescribable noise at times. Some of the Bedouins were sitting around a small fire at one side, and some of the children were having a little entertainment of their own on another side of the dancing party. We were soon satisfied, and made our way back to the hotel and laid down to rest.

The first Jericho was a walled city about two miles from the present village, perhaps at the spring already mentioned, and was the first city taken in the conquest of the land under Joshua. The Jordan was crossed at Gilgal (Joshua 4:19), where the people were circumcised with knives of flint, and where the Jews made their first encampment west of the river. (Joshua 5:2-10.) "Jericho was straitly shut up because of the children of Israel," but by faithful compliance with the word of the Lord the walls fell down. (Joshua 6:1-27.) "And Joshua charged them with an oath at that time, saying, Cursed be the man before Jehovah, that riseth up and buildeth this city Jericho: with the loss of his first-born shall he lay the foundation thereof, and with the loss of his youngest son shall he set up the gates of it." Regardless of this curse, we read that in the days of Ahab, who "did more to provoke Jehovah, the God of Israel, to anger than all the kings of Israel that were before him, * * * did Hiel the Beth-elite build Jericho: he laid the foundation thereof with the loss of Abiram his first-born, and set up the gates thereof with the loss of his youngest son Segub, according to the word of Jehovah, which he spake by Joshua the son of Nun" (1 Kings 16:33,34). "The Jericho * * * which was visited by Jesus occupied a still different site," says Bro. McGarvey. The present Jericho is a small Arab village, poorly built, with a few exceptions, and having nothing beautiful in or around it but the large oleanders that grow in the ground made moist by water from Elisha's Fountain. We had satisfactory accommodations at the hotel, which is one of the few good houses there. Jericho in the time of our Lord was the home of a rich publican named Zaccheus (Luke 19:1-10), and was an important and wealthy city, that had been fortified by Herod the Great, who constructed splendid palaces here, and it was here that "this infamous tyrant died." The original Jericho, the home of Rahab the harlot, was called the "city of palm trees" (Deut. 34:3), but if the modern representative of that ancient city has any of these trees, they are few in number. Across the Jordan eastward are the mountains of Moab, in one of which Moses died after having delivered his valedictory, as recorded in Deuteronomy. (Deut. 34:1-12.) From a lofty peak the Lord showed this great leader and law-giver a panorama of "all the land of Gilead unto Dan. * * * And Jehovah said unto him, This is the land which I sware unto Abraham, unto Isaac, and unto Jacob, saying, I will give it unto thy seed: I have caused thee to see it with thine eyes, but thou shalt not go over thither. So Moses the servant of Jehovah died there in the land of Moab, according to the word of Jehovah. And he buried him in the valley in the land of Moab, over against Beth-peor: but no man knoweth of his sepulchre unto this day."

Early Wednesday morning we began our toilsome journey back to Jerusalem, having nearly four thousand feet to climb in the twenty miles intervening. We stopped awhile at the Khan of the Good Samaritan, which stands near some old ruins, and may not be far from the place to which the Good Samaritan carried his poor, wounded fellow-man so long ago. Here I bought some lamps that look old enough, but may be quite modern imitations of the kind that were carried in the days of the wise and foolish virgins. A stop was also made at the Apostles' Fountain, near Bethany, where I saw an Arab working bread on his coat, which was spread on the ground. Over by the Damascus gate I one day saw a man feeding his camel on his coat, so these coarse cloth garments are very serviceable indeed. We got back to Jerusalem in time to do a good deal of sight-seeing in the afternoon.

The following Tuesday was occupied with a trip on "donkey-back" to Nebi Samwil, Emmaus, Abu Ghosh, and Ain Kairim. Our party was small this time, being composed of Mr. Jennings, Mr. Smith, the writer, and a "donkey-boy" to care for the three animals we rode, when we dismounted to make observations. He was liberal, and sometimes tried to tell us which way to go. We went out on the north side of the city and came to the extensive burial places called the "Tombs of the Judges." Near by is an ancient wine press cut in the rock near a rock-hewn cistern, which may have been used for storing the wine. En Nebi Samwil is on an elevation a little more than three thousand feet above the sea and about four hundred feet higher than Jerusalem, five miles distant. From the top of the minaret we had a fine view through a field glass, seeing the country for many miles around. This is thought by some to be the Mizpah of the Bible (1 Kings 15:22), and tradition has it that the prophet Samuel was buried here. A little north of Nebi Samwil is the site of ancient Gibeon, where "Abner was beaten, and the men of Israel, before the servants of David" (2 Samuel 2:12-17).

We next rode over to El Kubebeh, supposed by some to be the Emmaus of New Testament times, where Jesus went after his resurrection and sat at meat with his disciples without being recognized. (Luke 24:13-25.) The place has little to attract one. A modern building, which I took to be the residence of some wealthy person, occupies a prominent position, and is surrounded by well-kept grounds, inclosed with a wall. The Franciscan monastery is a good sized institution, having on its grounds the remains of a church of the Crusaders' period, over which a new and attractive building has been erected. One section of it has the most beautiful floor of polished marble, laid in patterns, that I have ever seen. It also contains a painting of the Savior and the two disciples.

We went outside of the monastery to eat our noon-day lunch, but before we finished, one of the monks came and called us in to a meal at their table. It was a good meal, for which no charge was made, and I understand it is their custom to give free meals to visitors, for they believe that Jesus here sat at meat with his two disciples. We enjoyed their hospitality, but drank none of the wine that was placed before us.

Our next point was Abu Ghosh, named for an old village sheik who, "with his six brothers and eighty-five descendants, was the terror of the whole country" about a century ago. Our object in visiting the spot was to see the old Crusaders' church, the best preserved one in Palestine. The stone walls are perhaps seven or eight feet thick. The roof is still preserved, and traces of the painting that originally adorned the walls are yet to be seen. A new addition has been erected at one end, and the old church may soon be put in repair.

The last place we visited before returning to Jerusalem was Ain Kairim, a town occupied mainly by the Mohammedans, and said to have been the home of that worthy couple of whom it was written: "They were both righteous before God, walking in all the commandments and ordinances of the Lord blameless" (Luke 1:6). The portion occupied by the Latins and Greeks is very beautifully situated on the side of the mountain. The stone houses, "whited walls," and green cypresses make quite a pretty picture. The Church of St. John, according to tradition, stands on the spot where once dwelt Zacharias and Elizabeth, the parents of John, the great forerunner of Jesus. Night came upon us before we got back to our starting place, and as this was my first day of donkey riding, I was very much fatigued when I finally dismounted in Jerusalem; yet I arose the next morning feeling reasonably well, but not craving another donkey ride over a rough country beneath the hot sun.

On Saturday, the twenty-second of October, I turned away from Jerusalem, having been in and around the place almost two weeks, and went back to Jaffa by rail. After a few miles the railway leads past Bittir, supposed to be the Beth-arabah of Joshua 15:61. It is also of interest from the fact that it played a part in the famous insurrection of Bar Cochba against the Romans. In A.D. 135 it was captured by a Roman force after a siege of three and a half years. Ramleh, a point twelve miles from Jaffa, was once occupied by

Napoleon. Lydda, supposed to be the Lod of Ezra 2:33, was passed. Here Peter healed Aeneas, who had been palsied eight years. (Acts 9:32-35.)

Jaffa is the Joppa of the Bible, and has a good deal of interesting history. When "Jonah rose to flee unto Tarshish from the presence of Jehovah," he "went down to Joppa and found a ship going unto Tarshish: so he paid the fare thereof, and went down into it, to go with them to Tarshish from the presence of Jehovah." (Jonah 1:3.) His unpleasant experience with the great fish is well known. When Solomon was about to build the first temple, Hiram sent a communication to him, saying: "We will cut wood out of Lebanon as much as thou shalt need; and will bring it to thee in floats by sea to Joppa; and thou shalt carry it up to Jerusalem" (2 Chron. 2:16). In the days of Ezra, when Zerubbabel repaired the temple, we read that "they gave money also unto the masons, and to the carpenters; and food, and drink, and oil, unto them of Sidon, and to them of Tyre, to bring cedar trees from Lebanon to the sea, unto Joppa, according to the grant that they had of Cyrus king of Persia" (Ezra 3:7). It was the home of "a certain disciple named Tabitha," whom Peter was called from Lydda to raise from the dead. (Acts 9:36-43.) Simon the tanner also lived in Joppa, and it was at his house that Peter had his impressive vision of the sheet let down from heaven prior to his going to Caesarea to speak the word of salvation to Cornelius and his friends. (Acts 10:1-6.)

The city is built on a rocky elevation rising one hundred feet above the sea, which has no harbor here, so that vessels do not stop when the water is too rough for passengers to be carried safely in small boats. Extensive orange groves are cultivated around Jaffa, and lemons are also grown, and I purchased six for a little more than a cent in American money. Sesame, wine, wool, and soap are exported, and the imports are considerable. The train reached the station about the middle of the day, and the ship did not leave till night, so I had ample time to visit the "house of Simon the tanner." It is "by the sea side" all right, but looks too modern to be impressive to the traveler who does not accept all that tradition says. I paid Cook's tourist agency the equivalent of a dollar to take me through the custom house and out to the ship, and I do not regret spending the money, although it was five times as much as I had paid the native boatman for taking me ashore when I first came to Jaffa. The sea was rough—very rough for me—and a little woman at my side was shaking with nervousness, although she tried to be brave, and her little boy took a firm hold on my clothing. I don't think that I was scared, but I confess that I did not enjoy the motion of the boat as it went sliding down from the crest of the waves, which were higher than any I had previously ridden upon in a rowboat. As darkness had come, it would have been a poor time to be upset, but we reached the vessel in safety. When we came alongside the ship, a boatman on each side of the passenger simply pitched or threw him up on the stairs when the rising wave lifted the little boat to the highest point. It was easily done, but it is an experience one need not care to repeat unnecessarily.

I was now through with my sight-seeing in the Holy Land and aboard the Austrian ship *Maria Teresa*, which was to carry me to the land of the ancient Pharaohs. Like Jonah, I had paid my fare, so I laid down to sleep. There was a rain in the night, but no one proposed to throw me overboard, and we reached Port Said, at the mouth of the Suez Canal, the next day.

CHAPTER VII.

EGYPT, THE LAND OF TOMBS AND TEMPLES.

The *Maria Teresa* landed me in Port Said, Egypt, Lord's day, October twenty-third, and at seven o'clock that evening I took the train for Cairo, arriving there about four hours later. I had no difficulty in finding a hotel, where I took some rest, but was out very early the next morning to see something of the largest city in Africa. The population is a great mixture of French, Greeks, English, Austrians, Germans, Egyptians, Arabians, Copts, Berbers, Turks, Jews, Negroes, Syrians, Persians, and others. In Smyrna, Damascus, and Jerusalem, cities of the Turkish empire, the streets are narrow, crooked, and dirty, but here are many fine buildings, electric lights, electric cars, and good, wide streets, over which vehicles with rubber tires roll noiselessly.

I first went out to the Mokattam Heights, lying back of the city, at an elevation of six hundred and fifty feet. From the summit an extensive view can be obtained, embracing not only the city of Cairo, with its many mosques and minarets, but the river beyond, and still farther beyond the Gizeh (Gezer) group of the pyramids. The side of the Heights toward the city is a vast quarry, from which large quantities of rock have been taken. An old fort and a mosque stand in solitude on the top. I went out by the citadel and passed the mosque tombs of the Mamelukes, who were originally brought into the country from the Caucasus as slaves, but they became sufficiently powerful to make one of their number Sultan in 1254. The tombs of the Caliphs, successors of Mohammed in temporal and spiritual power, are not far from the Heights.

As I was returning to the city, a laborer followed me a little distance, and indicated that he wanted my name written on a piece of paper he was carrying. I accommodated him, but do not know for what purpose he wanted it. I stopped at the Alabaster Mosque, built after the fashion of one of the mosques of Constantinople, and decorated with alabaster. The outside is full of little depressions, and has no special beauty, but the inside is more attractive. The entrance is through a large court, paved with squares of white marble. The floor of the mosque was nicely covered with carpet, and the walls are coated for a few feet with alabaster, and above that they are painted in imitation of the same material. The numerous lamps do much towards making the place attractive. The attendant said the central chandelier, fitted for three hundred and sixty-six candles, was a present from Louis Philippe, of France. A clock is also shown that came from the same source. The pulpit is a platform at the head of a stairway, and the place for reading the Koran is a small platform three or four feet high, also ascended by steps. Within an inclosure in one corner of the building is the tomb of Mohammed Ali, which, I was told, was visited by the Khedive the day before I was there.

The most interesting part of the day was the afternoon trip to the nine pyramids of the Gizeh group. They may be reached by a drive over the excellent carriage road that leads out to them, or by taking one of the electric cars that run along by this road. Three of the pyramids are large and the others are small, but one, the pyramid of Cheops, is built on such magnificent proportions that it is called "the great pyramid." According to Baedeker, "the length of each side is now seven hundred and fifty feet, but was formerly about seven hundred and sixty-eight feet; the present perpendicular height is four hundred and fifty-one feet, while originally, including the nucleus of the rock at the bottom and the apex, which has now disappeared, it is said to have been four hundred and eighty-two feet. * * * In round numbers, the stupendous structure covers an area of nearly thirteen acres."

It is estimated that two million three hundred thousand blocks of stone, each containing forty cubic feet, were required for building this ancient and wonderful monument, upon which a hundred thousand men are said to have been employed for twenty years. Nearly all of the material was brought across from the east side of the Nile, but the granite that entered into its construction was brought down from Syene, near Assouan, five hundred miles distant. Two chambers are shown to visitors, one of them containing an empty stone coffin. The passageway leading to these chambers is not easily traversed, as it runs at an angle like a stairway with no steps, for the old footholds have become so nearly worn out that the tourist might slip and slide to the bottom were it not for his Arab helpers. A fee of one dollar secures the right to walk about the grounds, ascend the pyramid, and go down inside of it. Three Arabs go with the ticket, and two of them are really needed. Those who went with me performed their work in a satisfactory manner, and while not permitted to ask for "backshish," they let me know that they would accept anything I might have for them. The ascent was rather difficult, as some of the stones are more than a yard high. It is estimated that this mighty monument, which Abraham may have looked upon, contains enough stone to build a wall around the frontier of France. Of the Seven Wonders of the World, the Pyramid of Cheops alone remains. The other attractions here are the Granite Temple, and some tombs, from one of which a jackal ran away as we were approaching. I got back to Cairo after dark, and took the eight o'clock train for Assouan.

This place is about seven hundred miles from Port Said by rail, and is a good sized town. The main street, fronting the river, presents a pleasing appearance with its hotels, Cook's tourist office, the postoffice, and other buildings. Gas and electricity are used for lighting, and the dust in the streets is laid by a real street sprinkler, and not by throwing the water on from a leathern bag, as I saw it in Damascus. The Cataract Hotel is a large place for tourists, with a capacity of three hundred and fifty people. The Savoy Hotel is beautifully located on Elephantine Island, in front of the town. To the south of the town lie the ancient granite quarries of Syene, which furnished the Egyptian workmen building material so long ago, and still lack a great deal of being exhausted. I saw an obelisk lying here which is said to be ninety-two feet long and ten and a half feet wide in the broadest part, but both ends of it were covered. In this section there is an English cemetery inclosed by a wall, and several tombs of the natives, those of the sheiks being prominent.

Farther to the south is a great modern work, the Nile dam, a mile and a quarter long, and built of solid masonry. In the deepest place it is one hundred feet high, and the thickness at the bottom is eighty-eight feet. It was begun in 1899, and at one time upwards of ten thousand men were employed on the works. It seemed to be finished when I was there, but a few workmen were still engaged about the place. The total cost has been estimated at a sum probably exceeding ten millions of dollars. There are one hundred and eighty sluices to regulate the out-flow of the water, which is collected to a height of sixty-five feet during the inundation of the Nile. The dam would have been made higher, but by so doing Philae Island, a short distance up the river, would have been submerged.

The remains on this island are so well preserved that it is almost a misnomer to call them ruins. The little island is only five hundred yards long and sixty yards wide, and contains the Temple of Isis, Temple of Hathor, a kiosk or pavilion, two colonnades, and a small Nilometer. In the gateway to one of the temples is a French inscription concerning Napoleon's campaign in Egypt in 1799. All the buildings are of stone, and the outside walls are covered with figures and inscriptions. Some of the figures are just cut in the rough, never having been finished. Here, as elsewhere in Egypt, very delicate carvings are preserved almost as distinct as though done but recently. The guard on the island was not going to let me see the ruins because I held no ticket. After a little delay, a small boat, carrying some diplomatic officers, came up. These gentlemen, one of whom was a Russian, I think, tried to get the guard to let me see the place with them, but he hesitated, and required them to give him a paper stating that I was there with them. Later, when I got to the place where the tickets were sold, I learned that Philae Island was open for visitors without a ticket. Perhaps the guard thought he would get some "backshish" from me.

I made an interesting visit to the Bisharin village, just outside of Assouan, and near the railroad. The inhabitants are very dark-skinned, and live in booths or tents, covered with something like straw matting. I stopped at one of the lodges, which was probably six feet wide and eight feet long, and high enough to enable the occupants to sit erect on the floor. An old man, naked from the waist up, was sitting outside. A young woman was operating a small hand mill, and one or two other women were sitting there on the ground. They showed me some long strings of beads, and I made a purchase at a low price. While at this lodge, for I can not call it a house, and it is not altogether like a tent, about a dozen of the native children gathered around me, and one, who could speak some English, endeavored to draw out part of my cash by repeating this speech: "Half a piaster, Mister; thank you very much." The girls had their hair in small plaits, which seemed to be well waxed together. One of the boys, about ten years of age, clothed in a peculiar manner, was finely formed, and made a favorable impression on my mind. I would like to see what could be made of him if he were taken entirely away from his unfavorable surroundings and brought up with the care and attention that many American boys receive. He and another lad went with me to see the obelisk in the granite quarry, and I tried to teach them to say: "Blessed are the pure in heart, for they shall see God." As I was repeating the first word of the sentence and trying to induce one of them to follow me, he said, "No blessed," and I failed to get either of them to say these beautiful words. In Egypt and other countries there are millions of persons just as ignorant of the gospel and just as much in need of it as the curly-headed Bisharin lad who conducted me to the granite quarry.

I took a pleasant boat ride across the river, past the beautiful grounds of the Savoy Hotel, to the rock tombs of the great persons of ancient Elephantine. I tarried a little too long at the tombs, or else did not start soon enough, for darkness came upon us soon after leaving them. For some distance the boatman walked on the shore and towed the boat with a long rope, while I tried to keep it off of the rocks with the rudder. There was not enough wind to make the sail useful, and as we were passing around the end of Elephantine Island we drifted against the rocks, but with no other loss than the loss of some time. It was my desire to see the Nilometer on the island, and I did see it, but not until after I had sent the boatman to buy a candle. This ancient water-gauge was repaired in 1870, after a thousand years of neglect. The following description by Strabo is taken from Baedeker's *Guide to Egypt*: "The Nilometer is a well, built of regular hewn stones, on the bank of the Nile, in which is recorded the rise of the stream—not only the maximum, but also the minimum, and average rise, for the water in the well rises and falls with the stream. On the side of the well are marks measuring the height for the irrigation and other water levels. These are published for general information. * * * This is of importance to the peasants for the management of the water, the embankments, the canals, etc., and to the officials on account of the taxes, for the higher the rise of the water, the higher the taxes." It needs to be said, however, that this "well" is not circular, but rectangular, and has a flight of steps leading down to the water.

On the way back to Cairo I stopped at Luxor, on the site of the ancient city of Thebes. The chief attraction here is the Temple of Luxor, six hundred and twenty-one feet long and one hundred and eighty feet wide. In recent times this temple was entirely buried, and a man told me he owned a house on the spot which he sold to the government for about four hundred and fifty dollars, not knowing of the existence of a temple buried beneath his dwelling. Some of the original statues of Rameses II. remain in front of the ruins. I measured the right arm of one of these figures, from the pit where it touches the side to the same point in front, a distance of about six feet, and that does not represent the entire circumference, for the granite between the arm and the body was never entirely cut away. Near by stands a large red granite obelisk, with carvings from top to bottom. A companion to this one, for they were always erected in pairs, has been removed. In ancient times a paved street led from this temple to Karnak, which is reached by a short walk. This ancient street was adorned by a row of ram-headed sphinxes on each side. Toward Karnak many of them are yet to be seen in a badly mutilated condition, but there is another avenue containing forty of these figures in a good state of preservation.

The first of the Karnak temples reached is one dedicated to the Theban moon god, Khons, reared by Rameses III. The Temple of Ammon, called "the throne of the world," lies a little beyond. I spent half a day on the west side of the river in what was the burial ground of ancient Thebes, where also numerous temples were erected. My first stop was before the ruins of Kurna. The Temple of Sethos I. originally had ten columns before it, but one is now out of place. The Temple Der el Bahri bore an English name, signifying "most splendid of all," and it may not have been misnamed. It is situated at the base of a lofty barren cliff of a yellowish cast, and has been partially restored.

In 1881 a French explorer discovered the mummies of several Egyptian rulers in an inner chamber of this temple, that had probably been removed to this place for security from robbers. In the number were the remains of Rameses II., who was probably reigning in the boyhood days of Moses, and the mummy of Set II., perhaps the Pharaoh of the Oppression, and I saw both of them in the museum in Cairo.

The Ramasseum is another large temple, built by Rameses II., who is said to have had sixty-nine sons and seventy daughters. There are also extensive remains of another temple called Medinet Habu. About a half a mile away from this ruin are the two colossal statues of Memnon, which were surrounded by water, so I could not get close to them. The following dimensions of one of them are given: "Height of the figure, fifty-two feet; height of the pedestal on which the feet rest, thirteen feet; height of the entire monument, sixty-five feet. But when the figure was adorned with the long-since vanished crown, the original height may have reached sixty-nine feet. * * * Each foot is ten and one-half feet long. * * * The middle finger on one hand is four and a half feet long, and the arm from the tip of the finger to the elbow measures fifteen and one-half feet."

All about these temples are indications of ancient graves, from which the Arabs have dug the mummies. As I rode out, a boy wanted to sell me a mummy hand, and another had the mummy of a bird. They may both have been counterfeits made especially for unsuspecting tourists. There are also extensive rock-cut tombs of the ancient kings and queens, which are lighted by electricity in the tourist season. I did not visit them on account of the high price of admission. The government has very properly taken charge of the antiquities, and a ticket is issued for six dollars that admits to all these ruins in Upper Egypt. Tickets for any one particular place were not sold last season, but tourists were allowed to visit all places not inclosed without a ticket.

While in Luxor I visited the American Mission Boarding School for Girls, conducted by Miss Buchanan, who was assisted by a Miss Gibson and five native teachers. A new building, with a capacity for four hundred boarders, was being erected at a cost of about thirty-five thousand dollars. This would be the finest building for girls in Egypt when finished, I was told, and most of the money for it had been given by tourists. I spent a night in Luxor, staying in the home of Youssef Saïd, a native connected with the mission work. His uncle, who could not speak English, expressed himself as being glad to have "a preacher of Jesus Christ" to stay in his house.

Leaving Luxor, I returned to Cairo for some more sight-seeing, and I had a very interesting time of it. In Gen. 41:45 we read: "Pharaoh called Joseph's name Zaphenath-paneah; and gave him to wife Asenath, the daughter of Potipherah, priest of On." Heliopolis, meaning city of the sun, is another name for this place, from whence the wife of Joseph came. It is only a few miles from Cairo, and easily reached by railway. All that I saw of the old city was a lonely obelisk, "probably the oldest one in the world," standing in a cultivated field and surrounded by the growing crop. It is sixty-six feet high, six feet square at the base, and is well preserved.

The Ezbekiah Gardens are situated in the best portion of Cairo. This beautiful park contains quite a variety of trees, including the banyan, and is a resort of many of the people. Band concerts are held, and a small entrance fee is taken at the gate.

On the thirtieth of the month I visited the Museum, which has been moved to the city and installed in its own commodious and substantial building. This vast collection of relics of this wonderful old country affords great opportunities for study. I spent a good deal of time there seeing the coffins of wood, white limestone, red granite, and alabaster; sacrificial tables, mummies, ancient paintings, weights and measures, bronze lamps, necklaces, stone and alabaster jars, bronze hinges, articles of pottery, and many other things. It is remarkable how some of the embalmed bodies, thousands of years old, are preserved. I looked down upon the Pharaoh who is supposed to have oppressed Israel. The body is well preserved, but it brought thoughts to me of the smallness of the fleshly side of man. He who once ruled in royal splendor now lies there in very humble silence. In some cases the cloths wrapped around these mummies are preserved almost perfectly, and I remember a gilt mask that was so bright that one might have taken it for a modern product. After the body was securely wrapped, a picture was sometimes painted over the face, and now, after the lapse of centuries, some of these are very clear and distinct. I saw a collection of scarabaei, or beetles, which were anciently worshiped in this country. Dealers offer figures of this kind for sale, but the most of them are probably manufactured for the tourist trade.

On Lord's day, October thirtieth, I attended the evening services at the American Mission, and went to Bedrashen the following day. This is the nearest railway station to Memphis, the ancient capital of Egypt, now an irregular pile of ruined mud bricks. I secured a donkey, and a boy to care for it and tell me where to go. We soon passed the dilapidated ruins of the old capital. Two prostrate statues of great size were seen on the way to the Step Pyramid of Sakkara, which is peculiar in that it is built with great offsets or steps, still plainly visible, although large quantities of the rock have crumbled and fallen down. The Department of Antiquities has posted a notice in French, Arabic and English, to the effect that it is dangerous to make the ascent, and that the government will not be responsible for accidents to tourists who undertake it. I soon reached the top without any special difficulty, and with no more danger, so far as I could see, than one experiences in climbing a steep hill strewn with rocks. I entered another pyramid, which has a stone in one side of it twenty-five feet long and about five and a half feet high. Some more tombs were visited, and the delicate carving on the inner walls was observed. In one instance a harvest scene was represented, in another the fish in a net could be discerned. The Serapeum is an underground burial place for the sacred bull, discovered by Mariette in 1850, after having been buried since about 1400 B.C. In those times the bull was an object of worship in Egypt, and when one died, he was carefully embalmed and put in a stone coffin in one of the chambers of the Serapeum. Some of these coffins are twelve feet high and fifteen feet long.

Before leaving Cairo, I went into the famous Shepheard's Hotel, where I received some information about the place from the manager, who looked like a well-salaried city pastor. The Grand Continental presents a better appearance on the outside, but I do not believe it equals Shepheard's on the inside. I was now ready to turn towards home, so I dropped down to Port Said again, where there is little of interest to the tourist except the ever-changing panorama of ships in the mouth of the Suez Canal, and the study of the social condition of the people. My delay in the city while waiting for a ship gave me a good deal of time for writing and visiting the missionaries. The Seamen's Rest is conducted by Mr. Locke, who goes out in the harbor and gathers up sailors in his steam launch, and carries them back to their vessels after the service. One night, after speaking in one of these meetings, I rode out with him. The American Mission conducts a school for boys, and Feltus Hanna, the native superintendent, kindly showed me around. The Peniel Mission is conducted by two American ladies. The British and Foreign Bible Society has a depot here, and keeps three men at work visiting ships in the harbor all the time. I attended the services in the chapel of the Church of England one morning. With all these religious forces the city is very wicked. The street in which my hotel was located was largely given up to drinking and harlotry.

On the ninth of November the French ship *Congo* stopped in the harbor, and I went down late in the evening to embark, but the authorities would not permit me to go aboard, because I had not been examined by the medical officer, who felt my pulse and signed a paper that was never called for, and I went aboard all right. The ship stopped at Alexandria, and I went around in the city, seeing nothing of equal interest to Pompey's Pillar, a monument standing ninety-eight feet and nine inches high. The main shaft is seventy-three feet high and nearly thirty feet in circumference. We reached Marseilles in the evening of November sixteenth, after experiencing some weather rough enough to make me uncomfortable, and several of the others were really seasick. I had several hours in Paris, which was reached early the next day, and the United States consulate and the Louvre, the national museum of France, were visited. From Paris I went to London by way of Dieppe and New Haven. I left summer weather in Egypt, and found that winter was on hand in France and England. London was shrouded in a fog. I went back to my friends at Twynholm, and made three addresses on Lord's day, and spoke again on Monday night. I sailed from Liverpool for New York on the *SS. Cedric* November twenty-third. We were in the harbor at Queenstown, Ireland, the next day, and came ashore at the New York custom house on the second of December. The *Cedric* was then the second largest ship in the world, being seven hundred feet long and seventy-five feet broad. She carries a crew of three hundred and forty, and has a capacity for over three thousand passengers. On this trip she carried one thousand three hundred and thirty-six, and the following twenty classes of people were represented: Americans, English, French, German, Danes, Norwegians, Roumanians, Spanish, Arabs, Japanese, Negroes, Greeks, Russian Jews, Fins, Swedes, Austrians, Armenians, Poles, Irish, and Scotch. A great stream of immigrants is continually pouring into the country at this point. Twelve thousand were reported as arriving in one day, and a recent paper contains a note to the effect that the number arriving in June will exceed eighty thousand, as against fifty thousand in June of last year. "The character of the immigrants seems to grow steadily worse."

My traveling companion from Port Said to Marseilles and from Liverpool to New York was Solomon Elia, who had kindly shown me through the Israelite Alliance School in Jerusalem. I reached Philadelphia the same day the ship landed in New York, but was detained there with brethren on account of a case of quinsy. I reached home on the fourteenth of December, after an absence of five months and three days, in which time I had seen something of fourteen foreign countries, having a very enjoyable and profitable trip.

CHAPTER VIII.

GEOGRAPHY OF PALESTINE.

This section of country has been known by several names. It has been called the "Land of Canaan," the "Land of Israel," the "Land of Promise," the "Land of the Hebrews," and the "Holy Land." Canaan was simply the country between the Mediterranean and the Jordan, extending from Mt. Lebanon on the north to the Desert of Arabia on the south. Dan was in the extreme northern part, and Beer-sheba lay in the southern end of the country, one hundred and thirty-nine miles distant. The average width of the land is about forty miles, and the total area is in the neighborhood of six thousand miles. "It is not in size or physical characteristics proportioned to its moral and historical position as the theater of the most momentous events in the world's history." Palestine, the land occupied by the twelve tribes, included the Land of Canaan and a section of country east of the Jordan one hundred miles long and about twenty-five miles wide, occupied by Reuben, Gad, and the half tribe of Manasseh. The Land of Promise was still more extensive, reaching from "the river of Egypt unto the great river, the river Euphrates," embracing about sixty thousand square miles, or a little less than the five New England States. The country is easily divided into four parallel strips. Beginning at the Mediterranean, we have the Maritime Plain, the Mountain Region, the Jordan Valley, and the Eastern Table-Land.

The long stretch of lowland known as the Maritime Plain is divided into three sections. The portion lying north of Mt. Carmel was called Phoenicia. It varies in width from half a mile in the north to eight miles in the south. The ancient cities of Tyre and Sidon belonged to this section. Directly east of Mt. Carmel is the Plain of Esdraelon, physically a part of the Maritime Plain. It is an irregular triangle, whose sides are fourteen, sixteen, and twenty-five miles respectively, the longest side being next to Mt. Carmel. Here Barak defeated the army of Sisera under Jabin, and here Josiah, king of Judah, was killed in a battle with the Egyptians under Pharaoh-necoh.

The Plains of Sharon and Philistia, lying south of Carmel, are usually regarded as the true Maritime Plain. Sharon extends southward from Carmel about fifty miles, reaching a little below Jaffa, and has an average width of eight miles. The Zerka, or Crocodile river, which traverses this plain, is the largest stream of Palestine west of the Jordan. There are several other streams crossing the plain from the mountains to the sea, but they usually cease to flow in the summer season. Joppa, Lydda, Ramleh, and Caesarea belong to this plain. Herod the Great built Caesarea, and spent large sums of money on its palace, temple, theater, and breakwater.

The Plain of Philistia extends thirty or forty miles from the southern limits of Sharon to Gaza, varying in width from twelve to twenty-five miles. It is well watered by several streams, some of which flow all the year. Part of the water from the mountains flows under the ground and rises in shallow lakes near the coast. Water can easily be found here, as also in Sharon, by digging wells, and the soil is suitable for the culture of small grains and for pasture. During a part of the year the plain is beautifully ornamented with a rich growth of brightly colored flowers, a characteristic of Palestine in the wet season.

Gaza figures in the history of Samson, who "laid hold of the doors of the gate of the city, and the two posts, and plucked them up, bar and all, and put them on his shoulders and carried them up to the top of the mountain that is before Hebron." Ashkelon, on the coast, is connected with the history of the Crusades. Ashdod, or Azotus, is where Philip was found after the baptism of the eunuch. It is said that Psammetichus, an ancient Egyptian king, captured this place after a siege of twenty-seven years. Ekron and Gath also belonged to this plain.

The ridge of mountains lying between the coast plain and the Jordan valley form the backbone of the country. Here, more than elsewhere, the Israelites made their homes, on account of the hostility of the inhabitants in the lowlands. This ridge is a continuation of the Lebanon range, and extends as far south as the desert. In Upper Galilee the mountains reach an average height of two thousand eight hundred feet above sea level, but in Lower Galilee they are a thousand feet lower. In Samaria and Judaea they reach an altitude of two or three thousand feet. The foot-hills, called the Shefelah, and the Negeb, or "South Country," complete the ridge. The highest peak is Jebel Mukhmeel, in Northern Palestine, rising ten thousand two hundred feet above the sea. Mt. Tabor, in Galilee, is one thousand eight hundred and forty-three feet high, while Gerizim and Ebal, down in Samaria, are two thousand eight hundred and fifty feet and three thousand and seventy-five feet respectively. The principal mountains in Judaea are Mt. Zion, two thousand five hundred and fifty feet; Mt. Moriah, about one hundred feet lower; Mount of Olives, two thousand six hundred and sixty-five feet, and Mt. Hebron, three thousand and thirty feet. Nazareth, Shechem, Jerusalem, and Hebron belong to the Mountain Region.

The Jordan Valley is the lowest portion of the earth's surface. No other depressions are more than three hundred feet below sea level, but the Jordan is six hundred and eighty-two feet lower than the ocean at the Sea of Galilee, and nearly thirteen hundred feet lower where it enters the Dead Sea. This wonderful depression, which includes the Dead Sea, forty-five miles long, and the valley south of it, one hundred miles in length, is two hundred and fifty miles long and from four to fourteen miles in width, and is called the

Arabah. The sources of the Jordan are one hundred and thirty-four miles from the mouth, but the numerous windings of the stream make it two hundred miles long. The Jordan is formed by the union of three streams issuing from springs at an elevation of seventeen hundred feet above the sea. The principal source is the spring at Dan, one of the largest in the world, as it sends forth a stream twenty feet wide and from twenty to thirty inches deep. The spring at Banias, the Caesarea Philippi of the Scriptures, is the eastern source. The Hashbany flows from a spring forming the western source. A few miles south of the union of the streams above mentioned the river widens into the waters of Merom, a small lake nearly on a level with the Mediterranean. In the next few miles it descends rapidly, and empties into the Sea of Galilee, called also the Sea of Chinnereth, Sea of Tiberias, and Lake of Gennesaret. In the sixty-five miles from the Sea of Galilee to the Dead Sea the fall is about six hundred feet. The rate of descent is not uniform throughout the whole course of the river. In one section it drops sixty feet to the mile, while there is one stretch of thirteen miles with a descent of only four and a half feet to the mile. The average is twenty-two feet to the mile. The width varies from eighty to one hundred and eighty feet, and the depth from five to twelve feet. Caesarea Philippi, at the head of the valley, Capernaum, Magdala, Tiberias, and Tarrichaea were cities on the Sea of Galilee. Jericho and Gilgal were in the plain at the southern extremity, and Sodom, Gomorrah, Admah, and Zeboim, upon which the wrath of God was poured, were somewhere in the region of the Dead Sea.

The Eastern Table-Land has a mountain wall four thousand feet high facing the river. This table-land, which is mostly fertile, extends eastward about twenty miles, and terminates in the Arabian Desert, which is still higher. Here the mountains are higher and steeper than those west of the Jordan. Mt. Hermon, in the north, is nine thousand two hundred feet high. South of the Jarmuk River is Mt. Gilead, three thousand feet high, and Mt. Nebo, lying east of the northern end of the Dead Sea, reaches an elevation of two thousand six hundred and seventy feet. Besides the Jarmuk, another stream, the Jabbok, flows into the Jordan from this side. The Arnon empties into the Dead Sea. The northern section was called Bashan, the middle, Gilead, and the southern part, Moab. Bashan anciently had many cities, and numerous ruins yet remain. In the campaign of Israel against Og, king of Bashan, sixty cities were captured. Many events occurred in Gilead, where were situated Jabesh-Gilead, Ramoth-Gilead, and the ten cities of the Decapolis, with the exception of Beth-shean, which was west of the Jordan. From the summit of Mt. Pisgah, a peak of Mt. Nebo, Moses viewed the Land of Promise, and from these same heights Balaam looked down on the Israelites and undertook to curse them, Moab lies south of the Arnon and east of the Dead Sea. In the time of a famine, an Israelite, named Elimelech, with his wife and sons, sojourned in this land. After the death of Elimelech and both of his sons, who had married in the land, Naomi returned to Bethlehem, accompanied by her daughter-in-law, Ruth, the Moabitess, who came into the line of ancestry of David and of the Lord Jesus Christ. Once, when the kings of Judah, Israel, and Edom invaded the land, the king of Moab (when they came to Kir-hareseth, the capital) took his oldest son, who would have succeeded him on the throne, "and offered him for a burnt offering upon the wall." At this the invaders "departed from him and returned to their own land."

The political geography of Palestine is so complicated that it can not be handled in the space here available. Only a few words, applicable to the country in New Testament times, can be said. The provinces of Galilee, Samaria, and Judaea were on the west side of the Jordan, while the Decapolis and Perea lay east of that river. The northern province of Galilee, which saw most of the ministry of Jesus, extended from the Mediterranean to the Sea of Galilee, and a much greater distance from the north to the south. It was peopled with Jews, and was probably a much better country than is generally supposed, as it contained a large number of cities and villages, and produced fish, oil, wheat, wine, figs, and flax. "It was in Christ's time one of the gardens of the world—well watered, exceedingly fertile, thoroughly cultivated, and covered with a dense population."—*Merrill.*

Samaria, lying south of Galilee, extended from the Mediterranean to the Jordan, and was occupied by a mixed race, formed by the mingling of Jews with the foreigners who had been sent into the land. When they were disfellowshiped by the Jews, about 460 B.C., they built a temple on Mt. Gerizim.

The province of Judaea was the largest in Palestine, and extended from the Mediterranean on the west to the Dead Sea and the Jordan on the east. It was bounded on the north by Samaria, and on the south by the desert. Although but fifty-five miles long and about thirty miles wide, it held out against Egypt, Babylonia, and Rome.

The Decapolis, or region of ten Gentile cities, was the northeastern part of Palestine, extending eastward from the Jordan to the desert. Perea lay south of the Decapolis, and east of the Jordan and Dead Sea. The kingdom of Herod the Great, whose reign ended B.C. 4, included all of this territory. After his death the country was divided into tetrarchies. Archelaus ruled over Judaea and Samaria; Antipas ("Herod the tetrarch") had control of Galilee and Perea; Philip had a section of country east of the Sea of Galilee, and Lysanius ruled over Abilene, a small section of country between Mt. Hermon and Damascus, not included in the domain of Herod the Great. Herod Agrippa was made king by Caligula, and his territory embraced all that his grandfather, Herod the Great, had ruled over, with Abilene added, making his territory more extensive than that of any Jewish king after Solomon. He is the "Herod the king" who killed the Apostle James and imprisoned Peter. After delivering an oration at Caesarea, he died a horrible death, "because he gave not God the glory." At his death, in A.D. 44, the country was divided into two provinces. The northern section was ruled by Herod Agrippa II. till the Jewish State was dissolved, in A.D. 70. He was the "King Agrippa" before whom Paul spoke. The southern part of the country, called the province of Judaea, was ruled by procurators having their seat at Caesarea. When Jerusalem was destroyed in A.D. 70, the country was annexed to Syria.

The climate depends more upon local conditions than on the latitude, which is the same as Southern Georgia and Alabama, Jerusalem being on the parallel of Savannah. In point of temperature it is about the same as these localities, but in other respects it differs much. The year has two seasons—the dry, lasting from the first of April to the first of November, and the rainy season, lasting the other five months, during which time there are copious rains. One authority says: "Were the old cisterns cleaned and mended, and the beautiful tanks and aqueducts repaired, the ordinary fall of rain would be quite sufficient for the wants of the inhabitants and for irrigation." The summers are hot, the winters mild. Snow sometimes falls, but does not last long, and ice is seldom formed.

Palestine is not a timbered country. The commonest oak is a low, scrubby bush. The "cedars of Lebanon" have almost disappeared. The carob tree, white poplar, a thorn bush, and the oleander are found in some localities. The principal fruit-bearing trees are the fig, olive, date palm, pomegranate, orange, and lemon. Grapes, apples, apricots, quinces, and other fruits also grow here. Wheat, barley, and a kind of corn are raised, also tomatoes, cucumbers, watermelons, and tobacco. The ground is poorly cultivated with inferior tools, and the grain is tramped out with cattle, as in the long ago.

Sheep and goats are the most numerous domestic animals, a peculiarity of the sheep being the extra large "fat tail" (Lev. 3:9), a lump of pure fat from ten to fifteen inches long and from three to five inches thick. Cattle, camels, horses, mules, asses, dogs and chickens are kept.

CHAPTER IX.
HISTORIC SKETCH OF PALESTINE.

In the ancient Babylonian city called Ur of the Chaldees lived the patriarch Terah, who was the father of three sons, Abram, Nahor, and Haran. Lot was the son of Haran, who died in Ur. Terah, accompanied by Abram, Sarai, and Lot, started for "the land of Canaan," but they "came unto Haran and dwelt there," "and Terah died in Haran." "Now Jehovah said unto Abram, Get thee out of thy country, and from thy kindred, and from thy father's house, unto the land that I will show thee: and I will make of thee a great nation, and I will bless thee and make thy name great; and be thou a blessing: and I will bless them that bless thee, and him that curseth thee will I curse: and in thee shall all the families of the earth be blessed." So Abram, Sarai, and Lot came into the land of Canaan about 2300 B.C., and dwelt first at Shechem, but "he removed from thence unto the mountain on the east of Bethel, and pitched his tent, having Bethel on the west and Ai on the east." Abram did not remain here, but journeyed to the south, and when a famine came, he entered Egypt. Afterwards he returned to the southern part of Canaan, and still later he returned "unto the place where his tent had been at the beginning, between Bethel and Ai. * * * And Lot also, who went with Abram, had flocks, and herds, and tents." On account of some discord between the herdsmen of the two parties, "Abram said unto Lot, Let there be no strife, I pray thee, between me and thee, and between my herdsmen and thy herdsmen; for we are brethren." Accepting his uncle's proposition, Lot chose the well watered Plain of the Jordan, "journeyed east," "and moved his tent as far as Sodom," but "Abram moved his tent, and came and dwelt by the oaks of Mamre, which are in Hebron."

Some time after this Chedorlaomer, king of Elam, entered the region occupied by Lot, and overcame the kings of Sodom, Gomorrah, Admah, Zeboiim, and Bela, carrying away the goods of Sodom and Gomorrah, "and they took Lot * * * and his goods." "And there came one that had escaped, and told Abram the Hebrew," who "led forth his trained men, born in his house, three hundred and eighteen, and pursued as far as Dan." As a result of this hasty pursuit, Abram "brought back all the goods, and also brought back his brother Lot, and his goods, and the women also, and the people." "The king of Sodom went out to meet" Abram after his great victory, and offered him the goods for his services, but the offer was refused. Abram was also met by "Melchizedek, king of Salem," who "brought forth bread and wine," and "blessed him." Before his death, the first Hebrew saw the smoke from Sodom and Gomorrah going up "as the smoke of a furnace," and he also passed through the severe trial of sacrificing his son Isaac. At the age of one hundred and seventy-five "the father of the faithful" "gave up the ghost, and died in a good old age, an old man and full of years, * * * and Isaac and Ishmael his sons buried him in the cave of Machpelah," at Hebron, where Sarah had been laid to rest when the toils and cares of life were over.

From Abraham, through Ishmael, descended the Ishmaelites; through Midian, the Midianites; and through Isaac, the chosen people, called Israelites, from Jacob, whose name was changed to Israel. The interesting story of Joseph tells how his father and brothers, with their families, were brought into Egypt at the time of a famine, where they grew from a few families to a great nation, capable of maintaining an army of more than six hundred thousand men. A new king, "who knew not Joseph," came on the throne, and after a period of oppression, the exodus took place, about 1490 B.C., the leader being Moses, a man eighty years of age. At his death, after forty years of wandering in the wilderness, Joshua became the leader of Israel, and they crossed the Jordan at Gilgal, a few miles north of the Dead Sea, capturing Jericho in a peculiar manner. Two other incidents in the life of Joshua may be mentioned here. One was his victory over the Amorites in the neighborhood of Gibeon and Beth-horon, where more were slain by the hailstones which Jehovah cast down upon them than were killed by Israel with the sword. It was on this occasion that Joshua said: "Sun, stand thou still upon Gibeon; and thou, Moon, in the valley of Aijalon. And the sun stood still, and the moon stayed, until the nation had avenged themselves of their enemies. * * * And there was no day like that before or after it." The other event is the complete victory of Israel over the immense army of Jabin, king of Hazor, fought at the Waters of Merom, in Galilee. The combined forces of Jabin and several confederate kings, "even as the sand that is upon the sea-shore in multitude, with horses and chariots very many," were utterly destroyed. Then came the allotment of the territory west of the Jordan to the nine and a half tribes, as Reuben, Gad, and the half tribe of Manasseh had been assigned land east of the river. The allotment was made by Joshua, Eleazer, the priest, "and the heads of the fathers' houses of the tribes of the children of Israel."

The period of the Judges, extending from Joshua to Saul, over three hundred years, was a time in which Israel was troubled by several heathen tribes, including the Moabites, Ammonites, Midianites, Amalekites, and Canaanites. The most troublesome of all were the Philistines, who "were repulsed by Shamgar and harassed by Samson," but they continued their hostility, capturing the Ark of the Covenant in the days of Eli, and finally bringing Israel so completely under their power that they had to go to the Philistines to sharpen their tools.

The cry was raised: "Make us a king to judge us, like all the nations." Although this was contrary to the will of God, and amounted to rejecting the Lord, the Almighty gave directions for making Saul king, when the rebellious Israelites "refused to hearken to the voice of Samuel," and said: "Nay, but we will have a king over us." Two important events in Saul's reign are the battle of Michmash and the war with Amalek. In the first instance a great host of Philistines were encamped at Michmash, and Saul, with his army, was at Gilgal. Samuel was to come and offer a sacrifice, but did not arrive at the appointed time, and the soldiers deserted, till Saul's force numbered only about six hundred. In his strait, the king offered the burnt offering himself, and immediately Samuel appeared, heard his explanation, and declared: "Thou hast done foolishly; thou hast not kept the commandment of Jehovah thy God. * * * Now thy kingdom shall not continue." Saul's loyalty to God was again tested in the affair with Amalek, and his disobedience in sparing Agag and the best of the cattle and sheep should be better known and more heeded than it is. Concerning this, the prophet of God chastised him, saying: "Behold, to obey is better than sacrifice, and to hearken than the fat of rams. For rebellion is as the sin of witchcraft, and stubbornness is as idolatry and teraphim. Because thou hast rejected the word of Jehovah, he hath also rejected thee from being king." The dark picture of Saul's doings is here and there relieved by the unadulterated love of Jonathan and David, "which, like the glintings of the diamond in the night," takes away some of the deepest shadows.

The next king, Jesse's ruddy-faced shepherd boy, was anointed by Samuel at Bethlehem, and for seven and a half years he reigned over Judah from his capital at Hebron. Abner made Ish-bosheth, the only surviving son of Saul, king over Israel, "and he reigned two years. But the house of Judah followed David." Abner, who had commanded Saul's army, became offended at the king he had made, and went to Hebron to arrange with David to turn Israel over to him, but Joab treacherously slew him in revenge for the blood of Asahel. It was on this occasion that David uttered the notable words: "Know ye not that there is a prince and a great man fallen this day in Israel?" Afterwards Rechab and Baanah slew Ish-bosheth in his bedchamber and carried his head to David, who was so displeased that he caused them to be killed, and their hands and feet were cut off and hanged up by the pool in Hebron. Then the tribes of Israel came voluntarily and made themselves the subjects of King David, who captured Jebus, better known as Jerusalem, and moved his capital to that city. During his reign the Philistines were again troublesome, and a prolonged war was waged against the Ammonites. During this war David had his record stained by his sinful conduct in the matter of Uriah's wife.

David was a fighting king, and his "reign was a series of trials and triumphs." He not only subdued the Philistines, but conquered Damascus, Moab, Ammon, and Edom, and so extended his territory from the Mediterranean to the Euphrates that it embraced ten times as much as Saul ruled over. But his heart was made sad by the shameful misconduct of Amnon, followed by his death, and by the conspiracy of Absalom, the rebellion following, and the death of this beautiful son. "The story of David's hasty flight from Jerusalem over Olivet and across the Jordan to escape from Absalom is touchingly sad. 'And David went up by the ascent of the Mount of Olives, and wept as he went up, and he had his head covered, and went barefoot.' Then what a picture of paternal love, which the basest filial ingratitude could not quench, is that of David mourning the death of Absalom, 'The king was much moved, and went up to the chamber over the gate, and wept: and as he went, thus he said, O, my son Absalom, my son, my son Absalom! would I had died for thee, O Absalom, my son, my son!'" After finishing out a reign of forty years, "the sweet singer of Israel" "slept with his fathers, and was buried in the city of David."

His son Solomon succeeded him on the throne, and had a peaceful reign of forty years, during which time the Temple on Mount Moriah was erected, being the greatest work of his reign. David had accumulated much material for this house; Hiram, king of Tyre, furnished cedar timber from the Lebanon mountains, and skilled workmen put up the building, into which the Ark of the Covenant was borne. This famous structure was not remarkable for its great size, but for the splendid manner in which it was adorned with gold and other expensive materials. Israel's wisest monarch was a man of letters, being the author of three thousand proverbs and a thousand and five songs. His wisdom exceeded that of all his contemporaries, "and all the earth sought the presence of Solomon to hear his wisdom, which God had put in his heart." A case in point is the visit of the Queen of Sheba, who said: "The half was not told me; thy wisdom and prosperity exceed the fame which I heard." But the glory of his kingdom did not last long. "It dazzled for a brief space, like the blaze of a meteor, and then vanished away." Nehemiah says there was no king like him, "nevertheless even him did foreign women cause to sin."

Solomon's reign ended about 975 B C., and his son, Rehoboam, was coronated at Shechem. Jereboam, the son of Nebat, whose name is proverbial for wickedness, returned from Egypt, whence he had fled from Solomon, and asked the new king to make the grievous service of his father lighter, promising to support him on that condition. Rehoboam counseled "with the old men, that had stood before Solomon," and refused their words, accepting the counsel of the young men that had grown up with him. When he announced that he would make the yoke of his father heavier, the ten northern tribes revolted, and Jereboam became king of what is afterwards known as the house of Israel. The kingdom lasted about two hundred and fifty years, being ruled over by nineteen kings, but the government did not run smoothly. "Plot after plot was formed, and first one adventurer and then another seized the throne." Besides the internal troubles, there were numerous wars. Benhadad, of Damascus, besieged Samaria; Hazael, king of Syria, overran the land east of the Jordan; Moab rebelled; Pul (Tiglath-pileser), king of Assyria, invaded the country, and carried off a large amount of tribute, probably amounting to two millions of dollars; and thirty years later he entered the land and carried away many captives. At a later date the people became idolatrous, and Shalmaneser, an Assyrian king, reduced them to subjection, and carried numbers of them into Assyria, and replaced them with men from Babylon and other places. By the intermarriage of Jews remaining in the country with these foreigners a mixed race, called Samaritans, sprang up.

The southern section of the country, known as the kingdom of Judah, was ruled over by nineteen kings and one queen for a period of about three hundred and seventy-five years. Asa, one of the good kings, was a religious reformer—even "his mother he removed from being queen, because she had made an abominable image for an Asherah; and Asa cut down her image and burnt it at the brook Kidron." But he, like many other reformers, failed to make his work thorough, for "the high places were not taken away: nevertheless the heart of Asa was perfect with Jehovah all his days." Joash caused a chest to be placed "at the gate of the house of Jehovah," into which the people put "the tax that Moses, the servant of God, laid upon Israel in the wilderness," until they had gathered an abundance of money, with which the house of God was repaired, for the wicked sons of Athaliah had broken it up and bestowed the dedicated things upon the Baalim. But after the death of Jehoida, the priest, Joash was himself led into idolatry, and when Zechariah, the son of Jehoida, rebuked the people for turning from God, they stoned him to death by the order of King Joash. The last words of the dying martyr were: "The Lord look upon it and require it." This is strangely different from the last expression of Stephen, who "kneeled down, and cried with a loud voice, Lord, lay not this sin to their charge." Amaziah returned "from the slaughter of the Edomites," and set up the gods of the idolatrous enemies he had whipped, "to be his gods." Ahaz was a wicked idolater, worshiping Baal and sacrificing his own sons.

In strong contrast with such men as these we have the name of Hezekiah, whose prosperous reign was a grand period of reformation and improvement. He was twenty-five years old when he came on the throne, and in the twenty-nine years he ruled, "he removed the high places, and brake the pillars, and cut down the Asherah." The brazen serpent, made by Moses in the wilderness, had become an object of worship, but Hezekiah called it "a piece of brass," and broke it in pieces. The passover had not been kept "in great numbers in such sort as it is written," so Hezekiah sent messengers from city to city to call the people to observe the passover. Some "laughed them to scorn, and mocked them," but others "humbled themselves, and came to Jerusalem," and in the second month the "very great assembly * * * killed the passover. * * * So there was great joy in Jerusalem; for since the time of Solomon the son of David, king of Israel, there was not the like in Jerusalem."

Manasseh, the next king, reëstablished idolatry, and his son Amon, who ruled but two years, followed in his footsteps. Josiah, who next occupied the throne, was a different kind of a man. "He did that which was right in the eyes of Jehovah, and walked in all the way of David his father, and turned not aside to the right hand or to the left." In his reign, Hilkiah the priest found the book of the law in the temple, and delivered it to Shaphan the scribe, who read it, and took it to the king and read it to him. "And it came to pass when the king heard the words of the book of the law, that he rent his clothes," and commanded that inquiry be made of the Lord concerning the contents of the book. As a result, the temple was cleansed of the vessels that had been used in Baal worship, the idolatrous priests were put down, the "houses of the sodomites," that were in the house of Jehovah, were broken down, the high places erected by Solomon were defiled, and a great reformation was worked.

Zedekiah was the last king in the line. In his day, Nebuchadnezzar, king of Babylon, invaded the land, and besieged Jerusalem for sixteen months, reducing the people to such straits that women ate the flesh of their own children. When the city fell, a portion of the inhabitants were carried to Babylon, and the furnishings of the temple were taken away as plunder. Zedekiah, with his family, sought to escape, going out over Olivet as David in his distress had done, but he was captured and carried to Riblah, thirty-five miles north of Baalbec, where his sons were slain in his presence. Then his eyes were put out, and he was carried to Babylon. In this way were fulfilled the two prophecies, that he should be taken to Babylon, and that he should not see it.

Thus, with Jerusalem a mass of desolate, forsaken ruins, the Babylonian period was ushered in. Some of the captives rose to positions of trust in the Babylonian government. Daniel and his three associates are examples. During this period Ezekiel was a prophet. No doubt the frame of mind of most of them is well expressed by the Psalmist: "By the rivers of Babylon, there we sat down, yea we wept when we remembered Zion. Upon the willows in the midst thereof we hanged up our harps."

The Medo-Persian period began with the conquest of Babylon by Cyrus, who brought the Jews under his rule. The captives were permitted to return to Palestine, and Zerubbabel soon had the foundations of the temple laid; but here the work came to a standstill, and so remained for seventeen years.

About 520 B.C., when Darius was king of Persia, the work was resumed, and carried on to completion. For some years the service of God seems to have been conducted in an unbecoming manner. Nehemiah came upon the stage of action, rebuilt the city walls, required the observance of the Sabbath, and served as governor twelve years without pay. Ezra brought back a large number of the people, repaired the temple, and worked a great reformation. Under his influence, those who had married foreign wives put them away, and "some had wives by whom they had children." As the Samaritans were not allowed to help build the temple, they erected one of their own on Mt Gerizim. A few Samaritans still exist in Nablus, and hold services on Gerizim. "After Nehemiah, the office of civil ruler seems to have become extinct."

The Greek period begins with the operations of Alexander the Great in Asia, 333 B.C., and extends to the time of the Maccabees, 168 B.C. After Alexander's death, his empire fell into the two great divisions of Egypt and Syria. The Egyptian rulers were called Ptolemies, and those of Syria were called the Selucidae. For one hundred and twenty-five years Palestine was held by Egypt, during which time Ptolemy Philadelphus had the Septuagint version of the Old Testament made at Alexandria. Syria next secured control of Palestine. The walls of Jerusalem were destroyed, and the altar of Jehovah was polluted with swine's flesh. We now hear of an aged priest named Mattathias, who at Modin, a few miles from Jerusalem, had the courage to kill a Jew who was about to sacrifice on a heathen altar. He escaped to the mountains, where he was joined by a number of others of the same mind. His death soon came, but he left five stalwart sons like himself. Judas, called Maccabeus, became the leader, and from him the whole family was named the Maccabees. He began war against the Syrians and apostate Jews. The Syrians, numbering fifty thousand, took up a position at Emmaus, while the Maccabees encamped at Mizpah. Although greatly outnumbered, they were victorious, as they were in another engagement with sixty thousand Syrians at Hebron. Judas entered Jerusalem, and repaired and cleansed the temple. Thus the Maccabean period was ushered in. After some further fighting, Judas was slain, and Simon, the only surviving brother, succeeded him, and Jerusalem was practically independent. His son, John Hyrcanus, was the next ruler. The Pharisees and Sadducees now come prominently into Jewish affairs. The Essenes also existed at this time, and dressed in white. After some time (between 65-62 B.C.), Pompey, the Roman general, entered the open gates of the city, but did not capture the citadel for three weeks, finally taking advantage of the day of Pentecost, when the Jews would not fight. The Roman period began with the slaughter of twelve thousand citizens. Priests were slain at the altar, and the temple was profaned. Judaea became a Roman province, and was compelled to pay tribute.

Herod the Great became governor of Galilee, and later the Roman senate made him king of Judaea. He besieged Jerusalem, and took it in 37 B.C. "A singular compound of good and bad—mostly bad—was this King Herod." He hired men to drown a supposed rival, as if in sport, at Jericho on the occasion of a feast, and in the beginning of his reign he slaughtered more than half of the members of the Sanhedrin. The aged high priest Hyrcanus was put to death, as was also Mariamne, the wife of this monster, who was ruling when the Messiah was born at Bethlehem. Herod was a great builder, and it was he who reconstructed the temple on magnificent lines. He also built Caesarea, and rebuilt Samaria. After his death, the country was divided and ruled by his three sons. Achelaus reigned ingloriously in Jerusalem for ten years, and was banished. Judaea was then ruled by procurators, Pilate being the fifth one of them, ruling from A.D. 26-36. In the year A.D. 65 the Jews rebelled against the Romans, after being their subjects for one hundred and twenty-two years. They were not subdued until the terrible destruction of the Holy City in A.D. 70, when, according to Josephus, one million one hundred thousand Jews perished in the siege, two hundred and fifty-six thousand four hundred and fifty were slain elsewhere, and one hundred and one thousand seven hundred prisoners were sold into bondage. The Temple was completely destroyed along with the city, which for sixty years "lay in ruins so complete that it is doubtful whether there was a single house that could be used as a residence." The land was annexed to Syria, and ceased to be a Jewish country. Hadrian became emperor in A.D. 117, and issued an edict forbidding the Jews to practice circumcision, read the law, or to observe the Sabbath. These things greatly distressed the Jews, and in A.D. 132 they rallied to the standard of Bar Cochba, who has been styled "the last and greatest of the false Messiahs." The Romans were overthrown, Bar Cochba proclaimed himself king in Jerusalem, and carried on the war for two years. At one time he held fifty towns, but they were all taken from him, and he was finally killed at Bether, or Bittir. This was the last effort of the Jews to recover the land by force of arms. Hadrian caused the site of the temple to be plowed over, and the city was reconstructed being made thoroughly pagan. For two hundred years the Jews were forbidden to enter it. In A.D. 326 the Empress Helena visited Jerusalem, and built a church on the Mount of Olives. Julian the Apostate undertook to rebuild the Jewish temple in A.D. 362, but was frustrated by "balls of fire" issuing from under the ruins and frightening the workmen. In A.D. 529 the Greek emperor Justinian built a church in the city in honor of the Virgin. The Persians under Chosroes II. invaded Palestine in A.D. 614 and destroyed part of Jerusalem. After fourteen years they were defeated and Jerusalem was restored, but the Mohammedans under Omar captured it in A.D. 637. The structure called the Dome of the Rock, on Mt. Moriah, was built by them in A.D. 688.

The Crusades next engage our attention. The first of these military expeditions was made to secure the right to visit the Holy Sepulcher. It was commenced at the call of the Pope in 1096. A force of two hundred and seventy-five thousand men began the march, but never entered Palestine. Another effort was made by six hundred thousand men, who captured Antioch in 1098. A little later the survivors defeated the Mohammedan army of two hundred thousand. Still later they entered Jerusalem, and Godfrey of Bouillon was made king of the city in 1099. By conquest he came to rule the whole of Palestine. The orders of Knights Hospitallers and Knights Templars were formed, and Godfrey continued in power about fifty years. In 1144 two European armies, aggregating one million two hundred thousand men, started on the second crusade, which was a total failure. Saladin, the Sultan of Egypt, conquered Jerusalem in 1187, and the third crusade was inaugurated, which resulted in securing the right to make pilgrimages to Jerusalem free from taxes. The power of the Crusaders was now broken. Another band assembled at Venice in 1203 to undertake the fourth crusade, but they never entered Palestine. The fifth effort was made, and Frederick, Emperor of Germany, crowned himself king of Jerusalem in 1229, and returned to his native land the next year. The Turks conquered Palestine in 1244 and burned Jerusalem. Louis IX. of France led the seventh crusade, another failure, in 1248. He undertook it again in 1270, but went to Africa, and Prince Edward of England entered Palestine in 1271 and accepted a truce for ten years, which was offered by the Sultan of Egypt. This, the eighth and last crusade, ended in 1272 by the return of Edward to England. In 1280 Palestine was invaded by the Mamelukes, and in 1291 the war of the Crusaders ended with the fall of Acre, "the last Christian possession in Palestine." Besides these efforts there were children's crusades for the conversion or conquest of the Moslems. The first, in 1212, was composed of thirty thousand boys. Two ship loads were drowned and the third was sold as slaves to the Mohammedans.

In 1517 the country passed to the control of the Ottoman Empire, and so remained until 1832, when it fell back to Egypt for eight years. The present walls around Jerusalem, which inclose two hundred and ten acres of ground, were built by Suleiman the Magnificent in 1542. In 1840 Palestine again became Turkish territory, and so continues to this day. The really scientific exploration of the land began with the journey of Edward Robinson, an American, in 1838. In 1856 the United States Consulate was established in Jerusalem, and twelve governments are now represented by consulates. Sir Charles Wilson created an interest in the geography of Palestine by his survey of Jerusalem and his travels in the Holy Land from 1864 to 1868. Palestine was surveyed from Dan to Beer-sheba and from the Jordan to the Great Sea in the years from 1872 to 1877. The Siloam inscription, the "only known relic of the writing * * * of Hezekiah's days," was discovered in 1880. The railroad from Jaffa to Jerusalem was opened in 1892. Within the last ten years several carriage roads have been built. Protestant schools and missions have been established at many important places. The population of the city is now about fifty-five thousand souls, but they do not all live inside of the walls. What the future of Palestine may be is an interesting subject for thought.

CHAPTER X.

CHURCHES OF CHRIST IN GREAT BRITAIN.

No doubt many of my readers will be specially interested in knowing something of my experience and association with the brethren across the sea, and it is my desire to give them as fair an understanding of the situation as I can. There are five congregations in Glasgow, having a membership of six hundred and seventy-eight persons. The oldest one of these, which formerly met in Brown Street and now meets in Shawlands Hall, was formed in 1839, and has one hundred and sixty-one members. The Coplaw Street congregation, which branched from Brown Street, and is now the largest of the five, dates back to 1878, and numbers two hundred and nineteen. It was my privilege to attend one of the mid-week services of this congregation and speak to those present on that occasion. I also met some of the brethren in Edinburgh, where two congregations have a membership of two hundred and fifty-three. At Kirkcaldy, the home of my worthy friend and brother, Ivie Campbell, Jr., there is a congregation of one hundred and seventy disciples, which I addressed one Lord's day morning. In the evening I went out with Brother and Sister Campbell and another brother to Coaltown of Balgonie, and addressed the little band worshiping at that place.

My next association with the brethren was at the annual meeting of "Churches of Christ in Great Britain and Ireland," convened at Wigan, England, August second, third, and fourth. While at Wigan I went out to Platt Bridge and spoke to the brethren. There are ninety members in this congregation. One night in Birmingham I met with the brethren in Charles Henry Street, where the congregation, formed in 1857, numbers two hundred and seventy-four, and the next night I was with the Geach Street congregation, which has been in existence since 1865, and numbers two hundred and twenty-nine members. Bro. Samuel Joynes, now of Philadelphia, was formerly connected with this congregation. While I was in Bristol it was my pleasure to meet with the Thrissell Street church, composed of one hundred and thirty-one members. I spoke once in their place of worship and once in a meeting on the street. The last band of brethren I was with while in England was the church at Twynholm, London. This is the largest congregation of all, and will receive consideration later in the chapter. The next place that I broke bread was in a little mission to the Jews in the Holy City. To complete a report of my public speaking while away, I will add that I preached in Mr. Thompson's tabernacle in Jerusalem, and spoke a few words on one or both of the Lord's days at the mission to which reference has already been made. I also spoke in a mission meeting conducted by Mr. Locke at Port Said, Egypt, preached once on the ship as I was coming back across the Atlantic, and took part in a little debate on shipboard as I went out on the journey, and in an entertainment the night before I got back to New York.

In this chapter I am taking my statistics mainly from the Year Book containing the fifty-ninth annual report of the churches in Great Britain and Ireland co-operating for evangelistic purposes, embracing almost all of the congregations of disciples in the country. According to this report, there were one hundred and eighty-three congregations on the list, with a total membership of thirteen thousand and sixty-three, at the time of the annual meeting last year.

(Since writing this chapter, the sixtieth annual report of these brethren across the sea has come into my hands, and the items in this paragraph are taken mainly from the address of Bro. John Wyckliffe Black, as chairman of the annual meeting which assembled in August of this year at Leeds. The membership is now reported at thirteen thousand eight hundred and forty-four, an increase of about eight hundred members since the meeting held at Wigan in 1904. In 1842 the British brotherhood numbered thirteen hundred, and in 1862 it had more than doubled. After the lapse of another period of twenty years, the number had more than doubled again, standing at six thousand six hundred and thirty-two. In 1902, when twenty years more had passed, the membership had almost doubled again, having grown to twelve thousand five hundred and thirty-seven. In 1842 the average number of members in each congregation was thirty-one; in 1862 it was forty; in 1882 it had reached sixty-one; and in 1902 it was seventy-two. The average number in each congregation is now somewhat higher than it was in 1902.)

Soon after the meeting was convened on Tuesday, "the Conference recognised the presence of Mrs. Hall and Miss Jean Hall, of Sydney, N.S.W., and Brother Don Carlos Janes, from Ohio, U.S.A., and cordially gave them a Christian welcome." The address of welcome and the address of the chairman, Brother James Anderson, of Fauldhouse, Scotland, came early in the day. The meeting on Wednesday opened with worship and a short address, followed by reports from the General Sunday-school, Reference, General Training, and Magazine Committees. One interesting feature of the proceedings of this day was the conference paper by Bro. T.J. Ainsworth on the subject of "The Relation of Christianity to the Social Questions of the Day." Besides a discussion of this paper, there was a preaching service at night. Thursday, the last day of the meeting, was occupied, after the morning worship and short address, with the reports of committees and the appointment of committees. At the social meeting at night several brethren, who had been previously selected, spoke on such subjects as seemed good to them. Bro. W.A. Kemp, of Melbourne, Australia, and the writer were the only speakers not residents of the British Isles. At the close of the meeting the following beautiful hymn was sung to the tune of "Auld Lang Syne":

Hail, sweetest, dearest tie, that binds
  Our glowing hearts in one;
Hail, sacred hope, that tunes our minds
  To harmony divine.
It is the hope, the blissful hope
  Which Jesus' words afford—
The hope, when days and years are past,
  Of life with Christ the Lord.

What though the northern wintry blast
  Shall howl around our cot?
What though beneath an eastern sun
  Be cast our distant lot?
Yet still we share the blissful hope
  His cheering words afford—
The hope, when days and years are past,
  Of glory with the Lord.

From Burmah's shores, from Afric's strand,
  From India's burning plain,
From Europe, from Columbia's land,
  We hope to meet again.
Oh, sweetest hope, oh, blissful hope,
  Which His own truth affords—
The hope, when days and years are past,
  We still shall be the Lord's.

No lingering look, no parting sigh,
  Our future meeting knows;
There friendship beams from every eye,
  And love immortal glows.
Oh, sacred hope, the blissful hope,
  His love and truth afford—
The hope, when days and years are past,
  Of reigning with the Lord.

I am not willing to accept everything done in the annual meeting, but the hearty good will manifested and the pleasant and happy associations enjoyed make it in those respects very commendable. These brethren are very systematic and orderly in their work. Some one, who has been designated beforehand, takes charge of the meeting, and everything moves along nicely. When a visiting brother comes in, he is recognized and made use of, but they do not turn the meeting over to him and depend upon him to conduct it. The president of the Lord's day morning meeting and part or all of the officers sit together on the platform. The following is the order of procedure in one of the meetings which I attended: After singing a hymn and offering prayer, the brother presiding announced the reading lessons from both Testaments, at the same time naming two brethren who would read these scriptures. After they had come forward and read the lessons before the church, another hymn was sung, and certain definite objects of prayer were mentioned before the congregation again engaged in that part of the worship. Two prayers were offered, followed by the announcements, after which a brother delivered an address. Then the president made mention of the visitors present, and an old gentleman from the platform extended "the right hand of fellowship" to some new members before the contribution was taken and the Lord's supper observed, a hymn being sung between these two items. A concluding hymn and prayer closed the service, which had been well conducted, without discord or confusion.

A brother in Wigan gave me a statement of the work of one of the congregations there in the winter season. On the Lord's day they have school at 9:20 A.M. and at 2 P.M.; breaking the bread at 10:30 A.M., and preaching the gospel at 6:30 P.M. At this evening meeting the Lord's table is again spread for the benefit of servants and others who were not able to be at the morning service. This is a common practice. The young people's social and improvement class meets on Monday evening, a meeting for prayer and a short address is held on Tuesday evening, and the Band of Hope, a temperance organization for young people, meets on Wednesday evening. The singing class uses Thursday night, and the officers of the church sometimes have a meeting on Friday night.

During the life of Bro. Timothy Coop much money was spent in an effort to build up along the lines adopted by the innovators here in America. Bro. Coop visited this country, and was well pleased with the operations of the congregations that had adopted the modern methods, and he was instrumental in having some American evangelists to go to England, and a few churches were started. I was told that there are about a dozen congregations of these disciples, called "American brethren" by the other English disciples, with a membership of about two thousand, and that it is a waning cause.

The rank and file of these British brethren are more conservative than the innovators here at home, but they have moved forward somewhat in advance of the churches here contending for apostolic simplicity in certain particulars. A few of the congregations use a musical instrument in gospel meetings and Sunday-school services, and some have organizations such as the Band of Hope and the Dorcas Society. The organization of the annual meeting is said to be only advisory. The following lines, a portion of a resolution of the annual meeting of 1861 will help the reader to form an idea of the purpose and nature of the organization: "That this Coöperation shall embrace such of the Churches contending for the primitive faith and order as shall willingly be placed upon the list of Churches printed in its Annual Report. That the Churches thus coöperating disavow any intention or desire to recognize themselves as a denomination, or to limit their fellowship to the Churches thus coöperating; but, on the contrary, they avow it both a duty and a pleasure to visit, receive, and coöperate with Christian Churches, without reference to their taking part in the meetings and efforts of this Coöperation. Also, that this Coöperation has for its object evangelization only, and disclaims all power to settle matters of discipline, or differences between brethren or Churches; that if in any instance it should see fit to refuse to insert in or to remove from the List any Church or company of persons claiming to be a Church, it shall do so only in reference to this Coöperation, leaving each and every Church to judge for itself, and to recognize and fellowship as it may understand the law of the Lord to require."

The question of delegate voting with a view to making the action of the annual meeting more weighty with the congregations was discussed at the Wigan meeting, but was voted down, although it had numerous advocates. One of the brethren, in speaking of the use of instrumental music in the singing, said they try not to use it when they worship the Lord, but I consider the use they make of it is unscriptural, and it puts the church in great danger of having the innovation thrust into all the services at some future time. All of these churches could learn a valuable lesson from some of our home congregations that have been rent asunder by the unholy advocacy of innovations.

But there are some very commendable things about these brethren. I noticed careful attention being given to the public reading of the Scriptures, and the congregation joins heartily in the singing. I am informed that every member takes part in the contribution without exception. They do not take contributions from visitors and children who are not disciples. The talent in the congregation is well developed. In this they are far ahead of us. While there are not many giving their whole time to evangelistic work, there are many who are acceptable speakers. One brother said they probably have a preacher for each twenty-five members. Men heavily involved in business take time to attend the meetings. For instance, one brother, who is at the head of a factory employing about a thousand people, and is interested in mining and in the manufacture of brick besides, is an active member of the congregation with which he worships. The brethren in general are faithful in the matter of being present at the breaking of bread. When visiting brethren come in, they are given a public welcome, and are sometimes pointed out to the congregation. Also, when brethren return from a vacation or other prolonged absence, they are given a welcome.

They pray much. The week-night meeting for prayer and study of the Bible is largely taken up with prayer. I like the way they point out definite objects of prayer. For instance, two sisters are leaving for Canada; some one is out of employment, and some have lost friends by death. These matters are mentioned, and some one is called on to lead the prayer, and these points are included in his petition to the Lord. Sometimes but one brother is asked to lead in prayer; sometimes more than one are designated, and at other times they leave it open for some one to volunteer. The following hymn was sung in one of these meetings which I attended:

LET US PRAY.

Come, let us pray; 'tis sweet to feel
  That God himself is near;
That, while we at his footstool kneel,
  His mercy deigns to hear;
Though sorrows crowd life's dreary way,
This is our solace—let us pray.

Come, let us pray; the burning brow,
  The heart oppressed with care,
And all the woes that throng us now,
  May be relieved by prayer;
Jesus can smile our griefs away;
Oh, glorious thought! come, let us pray.

Come, let us pray; the mercy-seat
  Invites the fervent prayer,
And Jesus ready stands to greet
  The contrite spirit there;
Oh, loiter not, nor longer stay
From him who loves us; let us pray.

They do not publish as many papers as we do, but have one weekly journal, the *Bible Advocate*, edited by Bro. L. Oliver, of Birmingham, which has a general circulation, reaching almost four thousand copies. One feature of the paper last summer was the publication of the Life of Elder John Smith as a serial. The colored covers of the *Bible Advocate* contain a long list of the hours and places of worship of congregations in different parts of the country, and even outside of the British Isles in some cases. In some instances the local congregation publishes a paper of its own, affording a good medium through which to advertise the meetings and to keep distant brethren informed of the work that is being done, as well as to teach the truth of God.

A book room is maintained in Birmingham, where the British and American publications may be purchased. They were using a hymn-book (words only) of their own and a tune-book published by others, but a new hymnbook was under consideration when I was among them last year. A list of isolated members is kept, and persons elected by the annual meeting conduct a correspondence with these brethren. The following are extracts from some of the letters received in reply to those that had been sent out: "I am hoping that the day will come when I can leave this district and get to one where I can have the fellowship of my brethren; but meanwhile I am glad and thankful to be held in remembrance of my brethren and to be on your list, and I pray God to help your work, for I have still hope in Him, and know He has not given me up." Another brother says: "Though I can not say that I have anything important or cheering to write, yet I can say that I am rejoicing in the salvation of God, which is in Christ Jesus our Lord. My isolation from regular church fellowship has been so long that I have almost given up the hope of enjoying it again in Arbroath; but still my prayer is that the Lord would raise up some here or send some here who know the truth, and who love the Lord with their whole heart, and would be able and willing to declare unto the people the whole counsel of God concerning the way of salvation." A Sisters' Conference was held in connection with the annual meeting, and a Temperance Conference and Meeting was held on Monday before the annual meeting opened.

Missionary work is being carried on in Burmah, Siam, and South Africa. In Burmah some attention has been given to translating and publishing a part of the Psalms in one of the languages of that country. "Much time has been spent in the villages by systematic visitation, by the distribution of literature, and by seizing upon any and every opportunity of speaking to the people. Street meetings have been constantly held, visitors received on the boat, the gospel preached from the Mission-boat to the people sitting on the banks of the river, and also proclaimed to the people in their homes, in the villages, and in the fields, and on the fishing stations. Although there were but two baptisms during the year the congregation numbers fifty-one." The brethren in Siam were working where the rivers, numerous canals, and creeks form the chief roadways. The Year Book contains the following concerning the medical missionary in this field: "His chief work during the year has been rendering such help as his short medical training has fitted him to give. For a time twelve to twenty patients a day came to him for treatment. After a while the numbers fell off, he thought because all the sick in the neighborhood had been cured." "The little church in Nakon Choom * * * now consists of two Karens, one Burman, one Mon, two Chinamen, and two Englishmen. As several of these do not understand the others' language, the gift of tongues would seem not undesirable." In South Africa there are congregations at Johannesburg, Pretoria, Bulawayo, Cape Town, and Carolina. The church in Bulawayo numbers about fifty members, nearly all of whom are natives "who are eager learners."

I saw more of the workings of the church at Twynholm than any other congregation visited, as I stayed at Twynholm House while in London both on the outward trip and as I returned home. Of the seven congregations in this city, Twynholm is the largest, and is the largest in the British brotherhood, having a membership of above five hundred. This church was established in 1894 with twenty-five members, and has had a good growth. They open the baptistery every Lord's day night, and very frequently have occasion to use it. There were fifty-three baptisms last year, and twenty-one others were added to the membership of the church. At the close of a recent church year the Band of Hope numbered five hundred and fifteen, and the Lord's day school had twelve hundred and fifty pupils and one hundred and two teachers. I think it was one hundred and sixty little tots I saw in one room, and down in this basement there were about fifty more. I was told that there were more children attending than they had accommodation for, but they disliked to turn any of them away. The Woman's Meeting had one hundred and sixteen members; the Total Abstinence Society, one hundred and fifty; and the membership of the Youths' Institute and Bible Students' Class were not given. Five thousand copies of *Joyful Tidings*, an eight-page paper, are given away each month. The following announcement from the first page of this paper will indicate something of the activities of this congregation:

CHURCH OF CHRIST,

Twynholm Assembly Hall,
Fulham Cross, S.W.

REGULAR SERVICES AND GATHERINGS.

LORD'S DAY.
9:45 A.M.—Bible Students' Class.
11:00 A.M.—Divine Worship and "The Breaking of Bread".
   (Acts 2:42, etc.)
2:45 P.M.—Lord's Day Schools.
3:00 P.M.—Young Men's Institute.
4:00 P.M.—Teachers' Prayer Meeting (first Lord's day in the
   month).
6:30 P.M.—*Evangelistic Service.*
7:45 P.M.—Believers' Immersion (usually).
8:10 P.M.—"The Breaking of Bread" (Continued).

MONDAY.
2:30 P.M.—Woman's Own Meeting.
7:00 P.M.—Band of Hope.
8:30 P.M.—Social Gathering for Young People (over fourteen).

8:30 P.M.—Total Abstinence Society (last Monday night in the month).

THURSDAY.

8:00 P.M.—Mid-week Service for Prayer, Praise, and Public Exposition of the Word.

9:00 P.M.—Singing Practice.

FRIDAY.

8:00 P.M.—Teachers' Preparation Class and Devotional Meeting. (Open to all).

Seat all Free and Unappropriated.
No Public Collections.
Hymn-books provided for Visitors.

This Church of Christ earnestly pleads for the complete restoration of the primitive Christianity of the New Testament, for the cultivation of personal piety, and benevolence, and for loving service for Jesus the Christ.

Twynholm is the name given to a piece of property, originally intended for a hotel, situated in the western part of London, at the intersection of four streets in Fulham Cross. These streets make it a place easily reached, and the numerous saloons make the necessity for such an influence as emanates from a church of God very great. There is a good, commodious audience-room at the rear, and several smaller rooms about the premises. The front part is owned and controlled by a brother who has a family of Christians to live there and run the restaurant on the first floor and the lodging rooms on the two upper floors, where there are accommodations for a few young men. Here I had a desirable room, and was well cared for by the brother and sister who manage the house. The restaurant is not run for profit, but to afford the people a place to eat cheaply and to spend time without going where intoxicants are sold. The patrons are allowed to sit at the tables and play such games as dominoes, the aim being to counteract the evil influences of that part of the city as far as possible. One night I attended a meeting of the Band of Hope in a big basement room at Twynholm, where a large number of small children were being taught to pray, and were receiving good instruction along the line of temperance. Several older persons were on duty to preserve order among these children, many of whom had doubtless come from homes where little about order and good behavior is ever taught. Soon after this meeting I went up on the street, and there, near a saloon with six visible entrances, a street musician was playing his organ, while small girls, perhaps not yet in their teens, were being encouraged to dance.

At Twynholm I also attended the Social Hour meeting, which was an enjoyable affair. A program of recitations, songs, etc., was rendered. This also, I suppose, is to offset some of the evil agencies of the great city and keep the young people under good influences. The Woman's Meeting convenes on Monday afternoon. The leaders of the meeting are ladies of the church, who are laboring for the betterment of an inferior class of London women. I spoke before this meeting, by request, and was, so far as I now recollect, the only male person present. It is the custom to use the instrument in connection with the singing in this meeting, but I asked them to refrain on this occasion. An orphans' home is also conducted, having members of this congregation as its managers. It is a very busy church, and for being busy and diligent it is to be commended, but I believe there is too much organization. But here, as elsewhere in Britain, there are many very commendable things about the brethren. I have already spoken of system in their proceedings. They outline their work for a given period of time, specifying the Scriptures to be read, the leaders of the meetings, and who is to preach on each Lord's day night. Then, for the sake of convenience, these schedules are printed, and they are carefully followed. This is far ahead of the haphazard method, or lack of method, at home, where brethren sometimes come together neither knowing what the lesson will be nor who will conduct the meeting.

Whatever may be the faults of these disciples in the old country, it must be said to their credit that they are kind and hospitable to strangers, and make a visiting brother welcome. The talent in their congregations is better developed than it is here, and their meetings are conducted in a more orderly and systematic manner. They are more faithful in the observance of the Lord's supper than many in this land. The percentage of preachers giving their whole time to the work is less than it is here, but the number who can and do take part in the public work of the church is proportionately larger than it is here.

I will now close this chapter and this volume with the address of Brother Anderson, chairman of the annual meeting held last year at Wigan:

DEAR BRETHREN:—In accepting the responsible and honorable position in which you have placed me, I do so conscious of a defect that I hope you will do your best to help and bear with. Please speak as distinctly as possible, so that I may hear what is said. There may be other defects that I might have helped, but please do your best to help me in this respect.

I heartily thank you for the honor conferred upon me. Whether I deserve it or not, I know that it is well meant on your part. We prefer honor to dishonor; but what one may count a great honor, another may lightly esteem. The point of view is almost everything in these matters; but if positions of honor in the kingdoms of the earth are lightly esteemed, positions of honor in the kingdom of God have a right to be esteemed more highly.

We are met in conference as subjects of the kingdom of God, as heirs of everlasting glory, having a hope greater than the world can give, and a peace that the world can neither give nor take away. To preside over such a gathering, met to consider the best means of spreading the Gospel of Christ among men, is a token of respect upon which I place a very high value. The fact that it came unexpectedly does not lessen the pleasure.

I know that you have not placed me here on account of my tact and business ability to manage this conference well. Had I possessed these qualities in a marked degree, you would no doubt have taken notice of them before this time. I know that you only wish to pay a token of respect to a plain old soldier before he lays aside his harness, and, brethren, I thank you for that.

For forty-four years I have enjoyed sweet and uninterrupted fellowship in this brotherhood. For over forty years my voice has been heard in the preaching of the Gospel of the Grace of God. For close on thirty years all my time has been given to the proclamation and defense of New Testament truth as held by us as a people. Every year has added strength to the conviction that God has led me to take my stand among the people who of all the people on the earth are making the best and most consistent effort to get back to the religion established by Christ and his apostles. I therefore bless the day that I became one of you.

Had our position been wrong, I have given myself every opportunity of knowing it. Circumstances have compelled me to examine our foundations again and again. I have been called upon to defend our faith, when attacked, times not a few. Whatever may be the effect that I have had upon others, my own confidence has been increased at every turn. To-day I am certain that if the New Testament is right, we can not be far wrong; and if the New Testament can not be trusted, there is an end to the whole matter. But the claims of Christ and the truth of the New Testament are matters upon which a doubt never rises. As years roll on, it becomes more easy to believe and harder to doubt. Knowledge, reason, and experience now supply such varied yet harmonious and converging lines of evidence that a doubt seems impossible. Difficulties we may have, and perhaps must have, as long as we live, but we can certainly rise above the fog land of doubt. Considering all this, it gives me more pleasure to preside over this gathering than over any other voluntary gathering on earth. It is a voluntary gathering. We do not profess to be here by Divine appointment. It is a meeting of heaven's freemen to consider the best means of advancing the will of God among men. While met, may we all act in a manner worthy of the great object which brings us together.

Faith, forbearance and watchfulness will be required as long as we live, if we wish to keep the unity of the faith in the bond of peace. All those who set out for a complete return to Jerusalem have not held on their way; some have gone a long way back and others are going. What has happened in other lands may happen here, unless we watch and are faithful. The more carefully we look into matters, we shall be the less inclined to move. Putting all God's arrangements faithfully and earnestly to the test, and comparing them with others, increases our faith in them. Faithfulness increases faith. This keeps growing upon you till you become certain that only God's means will accomplish God's ends. Sectarianism, tested by experience, is a failure.

The time was when our danger in departing from our simple plea of returning to the Bible alone lay in our being moved by clerical and sectarian influences. To the young in particular in the present day that can hardly be called our greatest danger. The influences at work to produce doubt in regard to the truth of the Bible were never so great as they are now. This used to be the particular work of professed infidels; now it is more largely the work of professed Christian scholars. If you wish to pass for a "scholar," you must not profess to believe the Old Testament. You must not say too much against the truth of that book, or you may be called in question, but you can go a good long way before there is much danger.

Jesus believed that old book to be the word of God. But he was not a "scholar." He was the son of a country joiner, and you must not expect him to rise too far above his environment. It surprises me that the "scholars" have not called more attention to the ignorance of Jesus in this respect. They will no doubt pay more attention to this later on; for as *Christian* "scholars" it becomes them to be consistent, and I have no doubt that they will shortly, in this respect, make up for lost time.

To expect that none of our young people will be influenced by this parade of scholarship is to expect too much. But faith in Christ should keep them from rushing rashly out against a book that Christ professed to live up to and came to fulfill. This battle of the scholars over the truth of the Bible is only being fought. We have no wish that it should not be fought. Everything has a right to be tested with caution and fairness, and when the battle is lost, it will be time enough for us to pass over to the side of the enemy. This question as to the truth of the Old Testament will be settled, and as sure as Christ is the Son of God, and has all power in heaven and on earth, it will be settled upon the lines of the attitude which he took up towards that book, and it will be settled to the disgrace of those who professed to believe in Jesus, but deserted his position before full examination was made. That no transcriber ever made a slip, or that no translator ever made a mistake, is not held by any one. But the day that it is proved that the Old Testament is not substantially true, faith in Christ and Christianity will get a shake from which it will never recover.

We have not lost faith in the Bible. There is no need for doing so. The word of the Lord will endure forever. But meantime, brethren, let us be faithful, prayerful, and cautious, and be not easily moved from the rock of God's word by the pretensions of "scholars" or of science, falsely so called.

I do not know that there is any necessary connection between the two, but a belief in evolution and scholarly doubts about large portions of the Old Testament, as a rule, go together. You must not profess to know anything of science in many quarters if you doubt evolution. In the bulk of even religious books it is referred to as a matter that science has settled beyond dispute. To expect that many of our young people will not be so far carried along by this current is to expect too much. Many of them will be carried so far; it is a question of how many and how far.

There perhaps never was a theory before believed by as many educated people without proof as the theory of evolution. It is an unproved theory; there is not a fact beneath it. That you have low forms of life, and forms rising higher and higher till you get to man, is fact. But that a higher species ever came from a lower is without proof. Let those who doubt this say when and where such a thing took place, and name the witnesses. Not only are there no facts in proof of it, but it flies in the face of facts without number. If like from like is not established, then nothing can be established by observation and experience. What other theory do we believe which contradicts all that we know to be true in regard to the subject to which it refers?

Not only does it contradict fact and experience, it contradicts reason. If you listen to the voice of reason, you can no more believe that the greater came from the less than you can believe that something came from nothing. We are intuitively bound to believe that an effect can not be greater than its cause. But the theory of evolution contradicts this at every step along the whole line.

I am anxious to find the truth in regard to anything that has a bearing upon my belief in God or religion. But in trying to find the truth, I have never regretted being true to myself. To slavishly follow others is, to say the least of it, unmanly. I do not believe in evolution because God has so made me that I can not. Wherever man came from, he sprang not from anything beneath him. When a man asks me to believe a thing that has not facts, but only theory to support it,—said theory contradicting fact, experience and reason,—he asks me more than I can grant. The thing is absurd, and must one day die.

I am agreeably surprised that we, as a people, have suffered so little as yet from the sources of error referred to. Still they are all living dangers, and if we would hold fast the faith once for all delivered to the saints, we must see to our own standing, and as God has given us opportunity let us be helpful to others. Our ground is God-given and well tested. The fellowship with God and with each other that it has brought to us has given us much happiness here. Let us be faithful and earnest the few years that we have to remain here, and our happiness will be increased when the Lord comes to reward us all according to our works.

———————

Milton Keynes UK
Ingram Content Group UK Ltd.
UKHW030742071024
449371UK00006B/630